Carl S. Dudley

Next Steps in Community Ministry
hands-on leadership

An Alban Institute Publication

The Publications Program of The Alban Institute is assisted by a grant from Trinity Church, New York City.

Library of Congress Catalog Card Number 95-83892
ISBN #1-56699-168-4

CONTENTS

AUTHORS

Titles are given for authors' present positions and for their former associations with the Church and Community Project.

Kimberly Bobo
Community Organizer, Midwest Academy
Advocacy Advisor, Church and Community Project

Philip C. Brown
Executive, Presbytery of Great Rivers, PCUSA
Regional Coordinator, Church and Community Project

John R. Buzza
Pastor, Hope Presbyterian Church, Springfield, Illinois
Hope for the Nineties Coordinator, Church and Community Project

Carl S. Dudley
Professor of Church and Community and Codirector of the Center
for Social and Religious Research, Hartford Seminary, Hartford,
Connecticut
Director of the Church and Community Project

David J. Frenchak
Executive Director, SCUPE, Seminary Consortium for Urban
Pastoral Care, Chicago, Illinois

Sally A. Johnson
> Executive Director, Chicago Metropolitan Mission of the
>   Evangelical Covenant Church
> Administrator and Research Associate, Church and Community
>   Project

Cathy A. Potter
> CFRE Library Development Officer, Purdue University
> Fund-Raising Consultant, Church and Community Project

Carl R. Smith
> Editor, *New Wineskins*
> Former Presbytery Executive, PCUSA

Susan E. Sporte
> Associate Professor, Framingham State College, Framingham,
>   Massachusetts
> Field Consultant and Research Associate, Church and Community
>   Project

Phil Tom
> Coordinator, Urban Ministries, Presbyterian Church (USA)
> Co-Director and Advocacy Consultant, Church and Community
>   Project

PREFACE

In many books the preface allows authors to acknowledge otherwise nameless people who contributed to the book. In this case the table of contents names ten, symbolic of the voices in a continuing dialogue between lay leaders, pastors, denominational staff, seminary faculty, and others who made almost a decade of the Church and Community Project so fascinating and productive.

With different takes on similar issues, the chapters reflect our conversations and mutual interests, even when we saw things differently. We speak not with the voice of a single author, but from intentionally different perspectives within a core of common experience. Beyond the voices of this book, we are grateful to all who joined as conversational partners in the Church and Community Project, more numerous than can be named in a single list.

We also acknowledge with appreciation many other partners who supported the project in a variety of ways. In particular we all thank Robert W. Lynn, Craig R. Dykstra, James P. Wind, and the board of the Lilly Endowment for encouraging, challenging, and funding this effort. Personally, I want to thank Sheryl Wiggins, Mary Jane Ross, and Shirley Sanford Dudley for recovering and reading several drafts, always reminding us that the final product should be useful to those in the front lines of community ministries.

Finally, to the faithful, courageous people in these churches who shared their experiences in developing and expanding community ministries in the face of shrinking resources, we offer our gratitude for all we and others can learn from your struggles.

INTRODUCTION

Carl S. Dudley

This book is about empowering congregations, especially the clergy and lay leaders who exercise their faith in developing community ministries. The findings of these chapters provide follow-up information on the earlier publication of *Basic Steps toward Community Ministry* (The Alban Institute, 1991), which detailed the initiation of thirty-two church-based social ministries through the Church and Community Project. Twenty-five ministries completed three years with the Church and Community Project in 1991. Five years later we can report on these ministries, their successes and deficiencies, their frustrations and discoveries.

Numerically, of the twenty-five ministries that set out on their own in the spring of 1991, twenty-four settled into a size they expect to maintain into the future—and one ministry for elderly people, that local leaders discontinued, has revived due to the extraordinary efforts of the participants themselves. This book is based primarily on research and interviews with these twenty-five continuing ministries.

Although these ministries generally work with small groups, the aggregate totals provide perspective on the group from whom we are learning. They serve more than three hundred preschool children, a thousand young people, and two thousand elderly people on a regular basis. They are involved with hundreds of families in all sorts of communities, from counseling to transitional shelters, from the renovation of dilapidated homes to new construction, from play space to family reunions. They employ only about thirty full-time and at least two hundred part-time staff, and there are more than a thousand volunteers. Their work is sponsored by at least fifty churches, and they work with at least an equal number of partner agencies, organizations, and local businesses.

Financially, most (eighteen of twenty-five) of their budgets exceed the seed funding ($20,000 annually). Since 1993, thirteen ministries have increased over 20 percent in budget, staff, and people served, and nine have increased between 30 percent and 50 percent, with two housing ministries generating million-dollar budgets. The total accumulated expenses from programs sponsored and sheltered by these ministries now approach $6 million annually. Recognizing that such a figure is disproportionately supported by the large budgets for housing and partnership programs, these ministries should be recognized at least as much for the high percentage of continuation (twenty-five of twenty-five with loss and gain), and the large number of individuals, congregations, and communities that are being touched every day throughout the two-state area.

But no ministry is average; each is unique and special to those who participate. In these pages we probe past the statistics to examine the nature of leadership—lay and clergy, individual and corporate—that enabled these community ministries to impact both the neighborhoods where they are located and the churches that supported them.

Background

The historical climate at the beginning of the project is relevant because it continues to be current. In the spring of 1986, as the federal government shifted financial resources away from local social services, Robert W. Lynn, vice president of the Lilly Endowment, indicated a willingness to fund a broad program of church-initiated social ministries. As members of a socially active church in the depressed east side of Indianapolis, Dr. Lynn and his wife, Kay, were impressed with the impact of hands-on community ministries both in the lives of community people and in the faith of church members. In that personal, local experience the Church and Community Project had its inception.

In 1987, we invited forty congregations in Indiana and Illinois to develop church-based community ministries. These congregations were Protestant and Catholic, mainline and evangelical, large and small, city and rural, Anglo, black, Hispanic, and Asian. Since these congregations roughly reflected the distribution of denominational churches in the two-state area and were not unusually committed to existing community ministries, we accepted them as a typical sample.

With Lilly resources we invited these local churches to rediscover their communities, identify needs, and launch community ministries. In 1988, thirty-two congregations initiated ministries for preschool children and teen parents, for latchkey rural kids and city kids on the streets, for adult literacy and crisis counseling, for home repairs and transitional housing, for elderly people in their homes and in community settings, for neighborhood organizations and community development.

In the process, we observed many changes. We saw volunteers transformed by their involvement in community concerns. We witnessed communities that felt empowered to act in their own behalf, to find assistance and demand a share in decisions about their lives. We saw congregations enlivened as members felt their faith was renewed when they touched the real pain of others and were touched by others in return. As one volunteer observed, "It hurts more when you see poverty in a person you call by name."

Working with so many congregations in a single project, we had a unique opportunity to see why and how churches became involved. Frankly, we were surprised to discover that all of the participating congregations—even ones that previously indicated low social concern, regardless of liberal or conservative theology, of large or small membership size, of social location or cultural composition—proved to have sufficient social, economic, and faith resources to sustain the development of successful programs of social ministry. Not demographics or theology, but leadership made the most significant difference between success and failure.

We learned that basic factors, such as theology, size, social location, and cultural composition, have a significant influence on what ministries churches choose and how they are developed. But these social conditions are not barriers that prohibit congregations from developing new community ministries—if the leaders are committed and the resources can be found.

Foundational Faith

The procedures we used in developing these ministries have been described in detail in our Alban publication of *Basic Steps toward Community Ministry*. In each church and community group, we invited leaders to combine three "basic steps": (1) to study their communities, (2) to acknowledge their congregational identity, and (3) to develop an organization to implement their decisions.

We found that clergy and laity were comfortable with this simple yet comprehensive framework for program development. Study of the social context was essential to provide the focus for ministry, while the congregational identity filtered the contextual information to enhance some community problems and ignore others. In addition, churches could not see what they did not believe they could change! Organizing for ministry gave leaders confidence that they could make a difference, and with that belief they saw their community with new eyes. Faith was their foundation for action.

From our experience we have written this book, focused on ten questions that we heard most frequently. From our front line participation with clergy and lay leaders, authors report their expectations, surprises, insights, and implications for the practice of ministry. We have divided these questions into four broad sections, with examples from the experiences and misperceptions that these ministries discovered in the process.

Part 1: Motivation

What moves volunteers in community ministries?

Volunteers who actively participated in social ministries were changed in the process. In chapter 1, Sally Johnson, Project Administrator and close friend to many of these ministries as they developed, details the transformation of volunteers as they became more informed and profoundly sensitive to needs of their neighbors. She shows how volunteers learned new responses and how the experience of volunteering increased their willingness to volunteer again. Strangers became friends, and statistics became real people who needed help.

Further, we discovered how volunteers found their personal faith enriched, and they saw the actual and potential of their own church in a new and more positive light. At the same time volunteers sometimes became discouraged—the problems seemed so huge, and the resources so meager. Experienced volunteers often pushed their churches to greater involvement as members experienced the pain of empathy: "The project has taught me the frustrations of the poor, and the impossible barriers against getting assistance from agencies that are paid to be helpful."

How did clergy make a difference?

In the second chapter, we identify some keys to clergy leadership as they share in developing these community ministries. Through the eyes of clergy, lay leaders, and outside observers, we noted the influence of pastors as they articulated the faith, facilitated the process, and became personally involved. We recorded significant differences in their styles of problem solving and resource development. With each task we explored the correlations between clergy style and project success.

Beyond the personal characteristics of every pastor, we found that leadership expectations and contributions are often rooted in denominational and cultural differences. But throughout the project we discovered that pastors were more effective when they recognized and chose their own style of leadership, and when they modified their choices to match the maturing sequence of each ministry.

How do pastors inspire new ministries?

In our surveys of social attitudes, the pastors consistently and significantly underestimated congregational support for community ministry. Typically, as noted above, clergy were more attracted to pastoral nurture than potential conflicts in developing community ministries. In the initial contact with congregations, half of the pastors expressed some fear of change, and a quarter of those contacted resisted involvement, saying, "My members would not support it." However, a strong minority of pastors wanted change and hoped that new ministries would help.

In the third chapter, David Frenchak, with a lifetime of educating urban clergy, reminds us of the importance of risk in responding to God's call. With a different reading of leadership opportunities, he offers hope for those who want both to nurture and to change the foundational roles for clergy. Rather than the old stereotypes of prophetic ministry, Frenchak suggests how visionary leaders have rewoven the boundary between church and community, strengthening both.

Part 2: Organization

How do churches organize these ministries?

There was not one successful way to organize; there were many. Some ministries were manager oriented and task centered. They wanted officers, clear goals, specific responsibilities, subcommittees with assignments, and job descriptions for personnel. They did it by the book.

But most did not follow any book in their organizational design, and they were equally successful. The most frequent organizing style was more casual, more like that of a family. Their core group was composed of friends and trusted community people who were comfortable working together. They decided by consensus, kept some records but not minutes, assigned duties to the most willing person, and expanded by asking another friend to join them.

In chapter 4, we consider a variety of organizational forms and the functional personalities, like the importance of "bridge" people who translate project expectations across racial and cultural differences.

Why do congregations approach social ministry so differently?

We found that congregations are mobilized into social ministries because members see their neighbors in need and respond with Christian compassion. Although in our initial contact with churches we invited proposals based on major social issues (namely, health, housing, employment, hunger, education, and world peace), we found that every proposal restated our issues as people with needs. For example, the churches named elderly people of their community who had health and housing problems; they saw youth with needs for education and employment.

In chapter 5, Carl Dudley and Sue Sporte examine the challenge of service and advocacy as an expression of congregational commitments. They suggest that most churches best energize ministry in ways that reflect their basic faith expressed in congregational character. They find that many ministries effect change simply by modeling a different and a better way, although at times confrontation with oppressive structures seems appropriate.

How can local churches advocate for social change?

We found that the ways that congregations personalize social issues create problems for leaders who are committed to justice ministries. The same compassion that responds to individuals may also be a barrier to seeing and changing the oppressive conditions that initially created the problems. Just as pastors are attracted more to nurture than to conflict, so laity are more inclined to service than to systemic change.

In chapter 6, Kim Bobo and Phil Tom, two old hands at organizing justice ministries among congregations, examine the experiences of participating churches. They show how a few congregations overcame their reluctance to challenge injustice, and they provide foundational guides for those who want to try. In the midst of confusion, they show hands-on ways for church leaders to focus on energizing issues and mobilize scarce resources.

Part 3: Resources

Where and how can we find money for ministry?

It can be done. The experience of Church and Community Project is bold testimony to the imagination and determination of church and community leaders, working together, to expand their resources. Although the Lilly Endowment provided several hundred thousand dollars in seed money to launch these thirty-two ministries, the continuing programs generated more than $3 million annually (see the appendix), three years after the financial supports were removed. When we repeated the process with other congregations but without the seed funding from Lilly, the ratio of success over failure increased, although the ministries were more modest in size.

In chapter 7, Cathy Potter, a professional fund-raiser with Purdue University Libraries, shares her experiences as a funding consultant in a wide range of church-based community ministries. Along with her procedures and suggestions, she tells of the courageous people who first met the fund-raising challenge "with fear and trembling" and, over time, have enjoyed the satisfactions of success, although the way is different from what they expected.

Can denominational staff be more than friendly strangers?

In a time of declining denominational loyalty and increasing local commitments, several times in the development of Church and Community
Ministries we gathered the related denominational leaders to explore
their professional roles, structural conditions, and personal experiences.
During nearly a decade in which these matured, they traced the expansion of local partnerships and a simultaneous decrease in the contacts and
commitment from denominational sources.

In chapter 8, Phil Brown and Carl Smith, two seasoned church executives, take a critical look at the changes that took place in personal
and professional relationships between the denominational leaders and
their churches that were developing community ministries. Even as
these authors confirm larger trends found elsewhere, they explore some
underlying tensions found in the spiritual journeys and structural settings
of denominational staff. On this basis they offer some alternative ways
of relating that might encourage new patterns of mutual support.

What about partners in ministry?

To have a lasting impact, most congregations need outside help in building a community ministry. Small congregations simply do not have all
the people, facilities, funding, and other resources essential for community ministry. Larger congregations may have more resources but poor
locations, and they often need connecting links to build strong community ministries. More than churches alone, other institutions, agencies,
and businesses can bring new energy, vision, and resources into a community ministry. Schools, banks, hardware stores, lumber yards, counseling agencies, government programs, and numerous other groups have
strengthened particular programs. But they come always with risk,
sometimes more expensive than anticipated.

Chapter 9 comes in two parts as separate authors provide different
perspectives on the potentials and liabilities of partners in community
ministries. As former project Administrator, Sally Johnson reports the
generic strengths and weaknesses of partners, but then explains a wide
variety of accommodations that helped individual projects make the most
of their unique conditions. As pastor of a congregation that expanded its

building to incorporate partner programming with four major social agencies, John Buzza provides a case study of struggle and achievement among partners for community ministries.

Part 4: Why, What, and How of Church and Community Ministries

Why did churches choose their social ministries?

In the process of developing new ministries, church members showed their faith in action and the values they hold most dear. By examining in chapter 10 the choices they made and the rationale they gave, we can help other congregations see the motives that move participation, and sometimes the complications that are involved. From that perspective they are all successes, since everyone made a good faith effort and all contributed to our storehouse of new understanding.

Appendix

Since we initially published the full list of participating churches in *Basic Steps toward Community Ministry*, this section provides a kind of "scorecard" on the condition of twenty-five (1 / 1) ministries nine years after we began the program in 1987 and almost five years after we completed seed funding in 1991. Written by Sue Sporte, former project Field Consultant, with Carl Dudley, former project Director, we offer a brief glimpse into the story of each ministry and numerical profile of programs, staff, volunteers, budget, participation, and the like.

Epilogue

Because these ministries provided a marvelous antidote to much of the negative thinking that sometimes surrounds commitment to social ministries, I highlight some of the helpful discoveries of leaders in these programs. The high rate of success in difficult times is a great tribute to the faith, creativity, and perseverance of the lay and clergy leaders who have unselfishly given themselves to construct and sustain these community ministries.

PART 1

Motivation

CHAPTER 1

Volunteer Satisfactions in Community Ministries

Sally A. Johnson

The strength or weakness of the church is the commitment of its members, the laity (*laos* in Greek, meaning *"the people"*). The muscles of community ministries are the volunteers who make it happen. In working with these ministries we found the faith and commitment of the people increased. Examples come from every project.

Two university students volunteered as tutors in an after-school program for low-income African-American children on Chicago's south side. Both had prepared for careers outside the field of education. As a result of their experience in the tutoring project, however, both enlisted in the Teach for America program. They are now in Los Angeles, teaching in an inner-city school.

A man of middle age in a small town was only marginally involved in his church when his pastor persuaded him to chair the core committee that organized their Church and Community Project. He soon became more actively involved in the church as well, including teaching an adult Sunday school class; and he is grateful that his pastor "shanghaied" him into this experience.

A young mother of four children lacked self-confidence because she did not have a college education; not recognizing her own gifts, she hesitated to take leadership roles in her church. Her pastor encouraged her to take an active part in their Church and Community Project, and she became codirector of the program; she was also elected chair of the congregation. She has now gone back to school to prepare for a career in teaching.

Although these are among the more striking cases of lives being changed by their involvement in a church-based social ministry, such stories are common. Volunteers find they gain as much from their work as do the people they seek to help. Pastors and lay leaders of social ministries should appreciate and build on these satisfactions.

In the Church and Community Project we have worked with a wide variety of volunteers—most of them church members. In thirty-two church-based ministry programs over nearly five years, we have observed not only what program leaders have done but also what it has meant to them. We have learned from them through frequent visits, phone conversations, and written reflections.

Formally, we surveyed leaders, volunteers, and staff of the Church and Community Projects. About 450 people filled out questionnaires, including nearly 200 who wrote comments in response to open-ended questions. The observations in this chapter are drawn from both of these sources—the broad profile given by the survey and the narrower, deeper focus provided by individuals' stories.

Our experience not only confirms what many pastors and laypeople have known intuitively for a long time about the positive effects of volunteering; it also sheds light on the nature of those effects and—perhaps most significantly—how churches can enhance this positive impact on people who work in ministry programs for the good of the church as well as the community.

What satisfactions do volunteers recognize?

On the broadest level, most volunteers feel good about their experience, and they feel good about all of it. On the survey we asked how much positive or negative impact they had found from their volunteer work in such areas as their confidence in their own leadership abilities, their awareness of social needs, and the depth of their religious commitments. Between 52 and 91 percent gave strong positive marks on each item, and no more than 5 percent responded negatively to any item. Some people found no change in particular areas. About one-fourth of the volunteers said they had not changed in nonreligious aspects of their experience (self-confidence, skills, and so on). In faith-related areas (increased personal commitment, greater involvement in their church, and so on) about one-third reported no significant changes from this experience. Most of the volunteers, of course, were church members with existing faith commitments that led them into community ministry.

Even though this group of volunteers did not differentiate much among the check-off items on the questionnaire, those who added comments gave strong insights into areas of particular impact for them. In addition to their written comments, we interviewed most of the participants in groups and individually. The patterns that emerge provide resources for leaders who invite and motivate participants in social ministries. Three clusters of responses reveal the most prominent ways in which volunteers acknowledge their satisfactions: awareness of community need, working relationships, and personal faith.

Awareness of Community Need

Volunteers most often talk of gaining a *greater awareness* of their community and its needs. One person wrote, "Seeing children from the... community has opened my eyes to the needs of groups that I have never come into contact with before, coming from a quite sheltered background." Another said, "I've become much more aware of the needs and problems of society in general. I've learned more and more that one person can make a difference." And another commented, "I am more aware of the people in my neighborhood as my neighbors and not just strangers living in the same area."

Furthermore, some talk about an increased *motivation to act* in response to the need. "This involvement brought to light a greater awareness of the needs and a greater commitment to giving to alleviate the needs," said one board member, and another reported, "This project has provided me a means of seeing the need firsthand and, more importantly, to do something about it." Some people become more involved in other social needs beyond the area of the immediate project: "I have just become more aware of the plight of the homeless, which has carried over into other concerns, i.e., mission"; and "Because of [this project] I started to teach as well as give of my time and money toward various social organizations."

For many volunteers, their work with a particular social ministry project makes them more deeply aware of the community and its needs, helps them to see their neighbors differently, and increases their active response to the immediate need and others.

Working Relationships

The second greatest benefit that volunteers speak of is the development
of *ecumenical relationships*. Often this is the first time they have shared
in ministry with neighboring churches. Some have never even been
inside other churches. "I discovered a lot more Christians in [town] than
I knew about!" said one person. "Confirms the belief I have that if a
person is a strong Christian it matters not what faith they are." And,
"[Our town] has not been as ecumenical as it could have been. The
[project] has made us work together."

A number of volunteers find satisfaction in the *personal friendships*
they develop through their work, regardless of the church affiliation.
One person spoke of "good fellowship one with another." "They are
dedicated, committed people and a joy to work with," said another, and
they were "affirming of others' gifts and abilities."

Other volunteers value broad *community cooperation*—churches and
other agencies working together for the common good. "The strong
positive impact," said one, "was that several members of the community
can join forces to address social concerns irregardless of religious
affiliation." Another person spoke of the "strong relationship between
the four agencies" cooperating in the project (including the church),
adding, "I think the community 'spirit' touches each life that is a part of
this project."

One Church and Community Project in a rural area set out to rebuild
this "community spirit" in its small town, reaching out to as many
different people as possible. Participants rallied support for a woman
who was not a member of either sponsoring congregation, in her attempt
to establish a small store in an abandoned gas station. Later they cared
for her personally when her husband became ill with cancer, mobilizing
volunteers to keep the store open during the long hours of his treatments.
Now a widow, this woman has turned down invitations to move elsewhere in order to remain in this community. She is an active leader in
the local project, and she writes the monthly community newsletter.

Sometimes *nonchurch volunteers* come to appreciate working with
church groups in community service. In the words of one person, "Because many of my experiences with organized religion have shown their
dogmatism and un-God-respecting behavior, I am honored and have deep
respect for individuals and organizations which are truly spiritually based

and respect and love human beings." Another was gratified to find that "a nonchurch member can work and participate in programs and projects without feeling like an outsider or being solicited to join."

And in some situations, volunteers learn and grow from developing relationships with people of other cultures. Whether the differences are ethnic, economic, or physical, learning to bridge them with mutual respect is a very positive experience. One person saw the group in a new way: "I became aware of the most serious lack of any understanding by Caucasian church groups of minority desires, needs, or culture." Another talked of "the incredible difficulties deaf people have in enjoying and taking advantage of the same freedoms that hearing people have."

Relationships are significant, then, in the kind of experience volunteers have in community ministry. They become more open to people of other faiths and cultures; they build community coalitions and personal friendships; and nonchurch neighbors come to see churches in a new and positive light, as partners in making their community a better place.

Faith

Volunteers tell of several ways in which their experience in community ministry has affected their faith. Some said that this work *deepened their own religious faith*: "My personal faith is stronger because of the commitment I made to [this project]," said one. "I believe more than ever in the miracle of Christ working in human lives." Another found affirmation in the success of the program: "Because of the financial stretch for both the agency and the church, and the fact that the project is working, my personal faith has been strengthened." And another said simply, "How could my faith fail to be deepened?"

Others speak from a more analytical perspective, saying this volunteer work has led them to *reflect, question, and redefine* their beliefs. One person commented, "Very increased awareness of the effects of poverty and violence on the children in this neighborhood has encouraged me to question and evaluate many of my own values." Another said, "When committed to a cause/project it changes your overall attitudes and behavior from what you previously had."

Some talk specifically about how their volunteer experience helped them to integrate faith and social ministry in their lives. Participating in the local Church and Community Project "helped me to clarify my thoughts on social justice issues and the role they play in religious beliefs," said one. Another talked of the need to "address the root causes of inadequate housing along with a continual faithful reflection of disciples," adding, "this dual commitment is what impacted me so strongly."

In devotion, reflection, and action, faith grows through sharing in community ministry. Not only do our commitments move us to reach out, but we are changed by that experience. A recently converted evangelical Christian, a recovering alcoholic and tavern owner, was invited onto the board of a local Church and Community Project, and a year later he was elected chair. Since then—through that role and others—his life has changed. He sold the tavern and took another job, and he plans to return to school and enter the professional ministry. When we set out to change things in our communities, often we ourselves are changed.

Other Responses

Another frequent response from volunteers is a greater sense of their own *leadership abilities*. Many people feel that their community work increases their skills and self-confidence. "[In] areas I had little experience in before, [this project] has given positive first experience on significant participation." "I never dreamed that I had leadership ability—I never dreamed it possible to achieve so much, so quickly, so joyfully, as it is when following God's will. I feel better about myself in whatever I try because of the newly discovered skills."

Some volunteers express a simple *satisfaction* in doing a good work. In one person's words, "This project has made me feel like I'm doing something to help, rather than just sitting back and saying, 'Oh, that's too bad.'" Others become more convinced of the importance of the *church's role in the community*. "I never really took time out to see how important the church is in the community," said one member. Some see more clearly the need for *advocacy* on justice issues. As one person said, "The project has really helped to make me aware of the frustrations of the poor and the difficulties in obtaining what is needed from systems that are supposed to be helpful."

Finally, like the man mentioned at the beginning of this chapter, some volunteers' *commitment to the church* increases as a result of their social ministry experience. One volunteer gave an example: "I became involved in this project through my work with the Board of Deacons, which led me to becoming president of the Deacons in 1990. I very willingly accepted this position due to the success I had with the Church and Community Project."

How can we increase the impact on volunteers?

As we came to realize how much their involvement in social ministry can affect volunteers, we began asking why the impact is so great in many cases. If churches could identify factors that enhance those effects, they could not only help individuals grow, but through them could also maximize their impact in the church.

Looking at the survey results, we sought connections between other circumstances and the strength of the positive effects that the volunteers reported.[1] Two factors emerged as especially important. Both relate to the pastor's role in particular, and by extension they show how the broader congregational context can help members to benefit the most from their experience.

The Pastor's Role

Volunteers reported that their pastors affected their growth through social ministry programs in two primary ways. First, pastors personally encouraged individual members to become involved in the community ministry program; and second, they preached a linkage between faith and social ministry from the pulpit. Overall, church members who had experienced either or both of those kinds of support from their pastors also reported greater positive impact in their own lives from their work.

This means that a pastor's work is not done when he or she has persuaded a volunteer to sign up. Rather, the pastor needs to follow and nurture the member throughout the work—and in doing so, the pastor can make a difference in the growth the member experiences. In giving voice to the theological foundations for faith expressed through social ministry, pastors give permission to volunteers to let their experience change them. In sermons and personal affirmations, pastors can articulate the experience and impact that the volunteers are feeling.

But going further, we suggest that this is not the pastor's job alone. The church's entire educational context should nurture the faith motivations for social involvement and also provide opportunities to tell and reflect on people's stories of doing community ministry. Susanne Johnson, in her book *Christian Spiritual Formation in the Church and Classroom*, notes that "it is necessary...to have some means of recognizing and expressing experience in order to have it" (Johnson 1989). When the sensations of personal involvement are named and claimed, they can be appropriated by the growing individual.

Changed People, Changed Churches

We have seen that volunteers in congregation-based social ministry programs can learn and grow from their work. In different ways and different degrees, an overwhelming majority of the volunteers we have observed say that their work has changed them for the better. People become more aware of and responsive to their communities. They form supportive and enriching relationships, often across lines encouraging for church leaders—some of them do grow in their individual faith lives through this volunteer ministry.

The good news is this: Not only can faith produce social ministry, but social ministry can produce—or at least enhance—faith. Leaders can build on the experiences of members to strengthen the church's social ministry. And when individual members experience the kinds of impact and growth that we have seen, they bring back with them seeds of renewal in the church as well.

---

[1]The analysis of this data was done by David P. Caddell, doctoral student at Purdue University and a research assistant for the Center.

CHAPTER 2

Clergy Contributions to Mobilizing Social Ministries

Carl S. Dudley

In response to my inquiries, a pastor voiced his lofty vision for his church's ministry, "Our understanding of the call to social ministry is founded on God's great compassion, the Kingdom, where the operating dynamic is love, and the character is peace and justice. The church is attempting to give to its community a glimpse of this Kingdom."

Almost by contrast, another pastor quietly invited members to continue the ministry of Jesus, "If we take the analogy of Paul concerning the church as the body of Christ seriously, then we realize we dare not leave those who suffer in any way to their own devices and resources. As we have heard in poetry and felt in our experience, we are 'His only hands, His only feet, and His only voice' that most people will ever know."

In the contrast between these two views many pastors struggle for the most appropriate way that they can help their members to explain and to embody the Christian faith. In developing community ministries pastors make a unique and significant contribution.

Pastors Must Respond to Many Leadership Demands

As spiritual leaders, clergy have many specific roles. They lead worship, preach, counsel, teach, plan, manage, console, pray, and continue countless other aspects of congregational care and nurture. In addition, pastors are expected to be organizers and catalysts for a wide variety of program activities from the intimacy of Bible study to socializing of basketball and bowling, from the fund-raising events to ministries of service and advocacy of change.

In this chapter we examine what clergy bring to organizing for ministries of compassion for people who are in need and justice for people who are oppressed. We recognize that social ministry is but one of many demands on clergy, but as shown in many parts of the Church and Community Project, social ministries can have a positive and lasting impact throughout many aspects of the congregation and the personal lives of numerous members.

From the outset we acknowledge a premise and a bias: Project guidelines provided that lay leaders, not pastors, must chair the organizing committees. This emphasis on lay leadership allowed the emerging ministries to be owned by the church (and their partners) and less limited to the pastor's agenda. Deprived of access to the clear and general role of the committee chair, the participating pastors had to articulate more specifically their leadership styles and often unconscious patterns. These foundational gifts of leadership became the focus of our study.

Team Player

Leadership is a group activity. Although the focus of this chapter is on the clergy, leadership is always complementary. Pastor and people bring a reservoir of wisdom and skill based on past experience and personal commitment. Ministry happens when clergy and laity mesh their strengths and compensate for their weaknesses in working toward a common end within the culture of the congregation. By naming these various roles, we hope to encourage both lay and clergy to identify and claim their roles in a parish leadership team.

To examine the special leadership contributions of clergy, we compiled interviews and observations on the work of forty-five pastors, gathered from the field consultants and staff of the Church and Community Project. Since these data come from people who were equally familiar with all the projects, but not intimately involved in any, we focus on comparisons among clergy styles employed by a variety of pastors in developing these community ministries.

From the wide assortment of descriptive language, we cluster the sup-portive work of clergy into five roles of ministry: *theologian*, who helps members know the faith rationale for the ministry; *vested authority*, who gives focus and direction to group decisions; *participant minis-*

ter, who leads by becoming directly involved in the ministry; *problem solver*, who helps process decisions in the group and individually; and *personal link*, who provides connections within and beyond this ministry.

Within each role, we note two different procedures or styles of ministerial leadership. The first style tends to be more visible with higher status in the seminary, while the second is often a lower profile but more accessible to clergy who see its value. Although one style may receive more acclaim, both high- and low-profile leadership styles are essential to launch and maintain new congregational programs.

Theologian

In the role of theologian, the pastor provides the rationale for engaging in every aspect of ministry. The theologian helps others recognize how God is at work in the world. Since social ministries happen at the intersection between the church and the world, a clear theological foundation provides the essential link between this particular activity and the larger mission of the church. The theological orientation clarifies why the church is engaged in this social ministry and how it fits within the congregation's Christian identity.

In a sense every believer is a theologian, and every task of leadership has a theological dimension—both to say and to live the way we believe God is at work in the world. The pastor's special responsibility is to pro-ide the workable language that makes sense to the members and inspires commitment to the task. We distinguish between the pastoral theologians who as *visionaries* raise the ideals and *theological coaches* who help group members say it for themselves.

Visionary pastors offer clear, compelling goals for the project, helping group members to imagine what they were attempting and to affirm their interest. Especially in the early stages of project development, the vision is essential for group cohesion and commitment. Visionaries often show the important links between the proposed ministry and congregational identity in their biblical faith traditions and in historic moments and leaders of the church. With vivid language and personal energy, visionary pastors can inspire strong commitment to a significant purpose. This gift is especially important in the initial phase and in times of uncertainty and transition.

Theological coaches are comparatively low key, but no less important—and coaches can get very excited in key moments of the game. So
much of the literature concentrates on theological visionaries that we
may overlook the importance of theologians who do not need to be so
articulate as long as they help the group to say it and claim it as their own.
Like the liturgist in worship, the theological coach helps volunteers to
unite their voices and their efforts in a task they do together. Some call
this task theological cheerleading—not the sweater girl who does somer-
saults, but the one with a megaphone who unites the voices of believers
with new energy to play the game.

In Bradford, Illinois, the Methodist system of rotating pastors
provided two such complementary theologians. Bradford is a quiet town
in a farming area with a regional high school and a single small industry.
In the initial stage of developing a social ministry, Pastor Dan of the
Methodist church rallied an ecumenical group around the dream of employing teenagers to help in the home maintenance of elderly people in
the community. He had the energy and early vision to bring the project
into a focus that invited others to join in the effort.

After the first year of ministry, Pastor Dan was replaced by Pastor
Bill, who brought very different leadership gifts. Bill is the essence of a
coach who helps others speak the faith and claim the project for their
own. Although the visionary pastor may receive more public attention,
people in the program reflect on their work with Bill's language and
insights. We cannot say how Dan or Bill might have acted if his place
had been changed, but the local ministry needed both the visionary and
the coach in the order they arrived.

Vested Authority

Authority is sometimes claimed by the office we hold or the skills we
offer. But we find that some congregations invest pastors with the authority to carry certain functions. We can identify two kinds of vested
authority. *Transformational pastors* are vested with the authority to
bring about significant change, and *traditional pastors* are equally en-
trusted to sustain the existing faith and rhythm of congregational life. In
both images, pastors recognize and use themselves as pivotal figures for
congregational unity in ministry.

Transformational pastors become the voice and embodiment of congregational decisions and activities, especially in critical moments of crisis and transition. In launching of social ministries, when these vested pastors spoke the word, it happened; and "the Lord saw that it was good." The Rev. Nathaniel Jarrett, pastor of Martin Temple AME Zion Church in Chicago, is aware that he carries the trust that members have vested in him, and he has used their confidence to help them invest several million dollars in a new center for worship and community service. Thoroughly convinced of the need for strong lay leadership, Nathaniel concludes, by the members' faith in him, he empowers them to greater heights.

A variety of churches vest clergy with transformative gifts. We find transforming pastors in a depressed urban neighborhood where three United Methodist churches have launched an assault to repair the deteriorating housing in their community, in a suburban Presbyterian church that embraced three nonchurch service agencies within the space of their building, and in an inner-city pentecostal Baptist church whose members have taken to street demonstrations against the oppressive power of drugs in the church's neighborhood. These trusted leaders are granted peculiar power to unify and mobilize their congregations.

Even more congregations invest their pastors with the authority to *maintain the faith traditions and program rhythms* of the church. In Canton, Illinois, the Rev. Roger Wentz is such a leader. The Canton ministry was launched by a more dramatic but less available pastor before Roger was called to lead the United Church of Christ. Roger joined as an early commitment in his new ministry. Now the energizing pastor who initiated this ministry has moved on to new ventures, while Roger remains the stabilizing and sustaining presence in inevitable storms of project development.

Not every church seems willing to support a transformational pastor, but every pastor who helps a ministry have roots becomes the bearer of tradition for that community. Transformational pastors are fewer with higher visibility, but pastors who symbolize continuity of core commitments are less controversial, highly honored, and essential to program maintenance through the years.

Participant Minister

Pastors who work directly with their projects approach the task in two
ways. Some are *delegating pastors* who seek others who might help
with the ministry, and the others are *servant pastors* who have the energy
and commitment to become personally involved, and some people do
both.

The *servant*, the worker bee, was the most frequent description of
pastors working with community ministries. For some pastors hands-on
participation is especially satisfying, even therapeutic, to relieve the administrative pressures of pushing papers on their desks. The Rev. Mollie
Clements of a Methodist parish in Indianapolis is symbolic of many. She
provides the vision for the project, and the members have vested strong
trust in her leadership. Yet since Mollie so enjoys becoming directly
involved in the work of ministry, she is primarily known throughout the
community as "one who lives her convictions."

By contrast, the Rev. David Smook, pastor of a two-hundred-member
rural congregation, is a good example of a *delegating pastor*. He might
have done the work himself; after two decades as pastor he knows what
should be done. But he prefers to be the "switchboard," connecting
people and tasks until he finds someone who is "right for the job." The
time gap between discovering a need and finding a willing worker is hard
for David, but he understands how long it takes to make decisions and
get commitments in the community. "Patience," he says, "is the key to
lasting action."

In reviewing the information on pastoral leadership, we note a problem in direct participation. Pastors in the Church and Community Project are twice as likely to be seen as servants than as delegators. The
projects, however, are twice as likely to be successful if the pastor is
effective in delegating the work to others.

Problem Solver

Pastoral leadership is evident in problem solving in two different ways.
Some pastors are *consultants*, entering projects to help solve specific
problems without necessarily retaining a seat on the working group.
Other pastors are *counselors*, preferring to focus more on the health of
individuals than the problems of the ministry as a whole.

The *consultants* have the skills to process issues but are not needed to manage the program. Rick Hull provided such service in the Mustard Seed Ministry, helping the board through its self-evaluation and goal-setting process. As pastor of the largest church in town, Rick gave status, direction, and renewed energy to the board without displacing its leadership or overburdening his schedule.

By contrast, *counselors* focus their pastoral skills on the needs of individual project leaders. As the pastor of a congregation sponsoring a community-wide advocacy ministry for people who are hearing impaired, the Rev. Cindi Hileman is a hearing person who knows American Sign Language. Cindi is a trusted counselor to whom people can turn in their frustration and anxiety. She is known as "the pastor" by church members and people who are deaf throughout the community. Without any formal office in the deaf ministry, she is essential to its stability, good spirit, and success.

The focus is different. Consultants help the group to achieve its goals while counselors focus primarily on the healthy functioning of individual group members. Although consultants may be more visible, both approaches demand a high level of professional skills, and both are greatly appreciated by the ministries they support.

Personal Link

Pastors provide a personal link in the development of ministries in two significant ways, one as a *bridge* between the church and the community, and the other as the *bond* within the core decision-making group.

As community leaders, pastors offer a *bridge* with a variety of connections between the church ministry and other community groups. Some pastors represent the project to the community as its voice and primary interpreter whether or not they are involved in its ongoing operations. From the pulpit and prayers to public meetings and press statements, these pastors can share the work of ministry even without directly belonging to the organization. Other pastors are more quietly bridging the work of ministry and the resources of the community by looking for new volunteers, seeking additional funds, and exploring new possibilities for program development. Since becoming involved in a community development program on the west side of Indianapolis, the Rev. John

Koppitch has become such a spokesperson for housing that the mayor appointed him to a municipal task force. In his many community contacts, the pastor has given the ministry significant media attention and has generated substantial amounts of new funding for the ministry.

In their perspective from within a project, some pastors become the *bond* that holds the participants together in good times and in hard times. Pastors do not need to be chair or treasurer or any elevated office. For at least half of the pastors, their greatest gift was their sustaining presence. "They were always there when we needed them," reported appreciative members. Grateful project leaders counted on pastors who carried them through the long, dry, difficult periods of shaping and sustaining various ministries.

Pastors Should Use Their Leadership Styles

Many elements contribute to members' expectations for their clergy leaders, including denominational background, cultural heritage, educational level, employment experiences and, of course, the pastor's background and personhood. In this overview of pastoral leadership we affirm these unique influences, yet suggest a few guidelines that might be drawn from our more general study to help pastors strengthen their pastoral styles and increase their effectiveness.

1. *Pastors should know their own gifts and limitations.* In some roles pastors are the primary actors. In offering vision, urging transformation, and bridging to community groups, for example, pastors typically take the initiative. In other roles pastors facilitate the group. As theological coach, pastoral counselor, and source of bonding, pastors play a significant role within the leadership group.

Some pastors are more gifted outside the program, some are more comfortable within, and some do both with equal ease. After reviewing the many significant roles that pastors play, we reject a hierarchy of gifts, but we affirm the importance of timing. At some moments in the sequence of development certain gifts are more useful, but the needs change with time. We often wished that pastors knew their gifts and used them when appropriate, rather than expecting that the situation would automatically match their gifts, or maintaining a style after it had served its purpose.

2. *Pastors should negotiate leadership styles in cultural context.*
Every pastor, every lay leader, and every congregation has gifts and limitations. When we approach congregational leadership as a team, where
all players bring gifts for the common cause, laity and clergy can work
together to find the role each will play and the style each will use to
reach their goals.

The pastoral leadership, for example, must fit the expectations of
congregational culture. Congregations of African-American and other
strong ethnic identities tend to vest their leaders with more authority.
Small churches tend to be more informal and organize through familylike
networks of people who know each other well. Rural churches of any
size tend to operate like extended families. Working together, pastors
and lay leaders can stake out the territory and adjust their approach to
maximize their contributions.

3. *Pastoral leadership should match project development.* In organizing community ministries we found a great difference between
launching and maintaining the ministry. Like the physics of inertia, programs require more effort and focus in the initial phase and in times of
transition, especially in crises. Indeed, crises may be defined as lack of
commitment to the status quo.

For this reason pastors often need to give more energy in start-up and
transition as compared with lower energy but solid support to maintain a
continuing ministry.

4. *Pastoral leaders can be barriers to ministry.* Although rarely
discussed in print, all of these positive contributions of clergy can be
detrimental when carried to extremes. Visionary theologians can create
a world of their own, and vested leaders can become manipulative and
controlling. Servants can displace other workers, sometimes creating
crippling dependencies.

Some pastors are seen as entrepreneurs in ministry, more concerned
with building a program than helping people. Others become negative,
expecting failure, draining precious energy. Some pastors become de-
tached or competitive about the success of the community ministry as
compared with other aspects of the church. When leadership gifts are
exaggerated to an extreme, they often inhibit pastoral effectiveness.

5. *Pastoral leaders should be clear and consistent.* Unlike any other
participants, pastors have a unique relationship to social ministries sponsored by their churches. They have a voice even if they do not have an

official position or attend meetings. Within the group they can bring vision and energy, continuity and change, new volunteers and problem-solving skills. Beyond the group they can interpret the ministry, provide links to other community groups, and generate necessary resources.

Pastors have an amazing variety of contributions that can assist developing ministries. There is no formula that assures success, but pastoral opposition is fatal, and unexpected inconsistencies are damaging. There seems no limit, however, to the wide and wonderful variety of combinations of gifts that can be productive when lay and clergy team up in a commitment to develop strong new ministries to express their faith in action.

CHAPTER 3

Visionary Leadership in Launching Social Ministries

David J. Frenchak

In the dynamics of congregational leadership, visionary leaders are crucial to the structure, process, and implementation of social ministries in congregations. The Church and Community Project has identified three "critical elements" necessary for congregations that wish to be socially involved in their communities—tradition, organization, and inspiration. In every successful project we would expect to find advocates for tradition, an administrative committee, and a visionary leader who is the essential source of inspiration.

From its inception the Church and Community Project recognized that while congregations may differ, representatives of all three of the critical elements should be present in each ministry. Project leaders did not expect that a person functioning in a particular role or position would either assume or be limited to a single leadership function. In practice the lay committee chair might be the visionary leader, the pastor might be the administrative leader, and a third person or group might assume responsibility for history and tradition, or some other combination, including individuals who filled multiple leadership roles.

Such a project design invites a special study on the unique role of the visionary leader alone, and the dynamics created when such leadership is accompanied by an equal emphasis on organizational structure and encumbered with historical memories. More specifically, the traditional but contemporary church must wrestle with the question, What is the place for the visionary leader in congregational planning for ministry?

Clearly, visionary leaders have a significant role and force in social ministries both nationally and locally, particularly ministries of justice as well as service. Because of the centrality and significance of visionary leaders in social ministry across the globe, and because the Church and Community Project intentionally created a space for visionary leadership, we have a unique opportunity to examine visionary leadership in the development of social ministries.

Assuming Leadership

For a working definition, the visionary leader is someone who assumes responsibility for transforming reality and practices the art of getting others to want to contribute to the transformation. This simple definition highlights several essential aspects of visionary leadership. The visionary leader *assumes* the right to make things happen. Most often the visionary leader does not wait for either appointment or invitation to leadership. Position and/or title, either assigned or acquired, is secondary to "the calling" for the visionary leader. This sense of calling enables the visionary leader to assume rights and roles.

The visionary leader often functions from a claim to an authority outside himself or herself, a higher authority. This claim draws attention to a dimension of spiritual authority inherent in visionary leadership. The visionary leader's charisma is a direct outgrowth of the belief that she or he has a personal calling to make a difference in the way things are seen and done.

The visionary leader is not simply responding to a job description, agreeing with an organizational mission statement, or merely accepting a role. *The call* is the source of energy and power because it is understood by the visionary leader as coming from outside himself or herself. It provides the authority. When empowered by a call, the visionary leader must respond. Empowered by this conviction, the leader shares the vision. The message typically includes a strong sense of destiny that informs time, task, challenge, and behavior not only for the leader but also for all those who share the vision.

Since this sense of a strong spiritual call is integral to visionary leadership, we must recognize the potential for social and religious abuse. This reality of such potential abuse, however, will neither deter the political activity nor negate the power experienced in a leader who has a sense of call from God and who connects that call with a sense of destiny.

Change is an equally important dimension embedded in this definition of a visionary leader. Tension between visionary leadership and
management leadership most often generates around this dimension.
This is particularly true when management controls and maintains the
status quo. However, by definition visionary leaders bring change because they assume responsibility to make change happen. The conflict
between visionary leadership and management leadership was evidenced
in the '92 presidential campaign. Change was the campaign theme of the
liberal candidate for president, while the conservative presidential candidate scoffed at change, saying, "What is this vision stuff?"

Transforming Reality

Third, and perhaps most important, the visionary or transformative leader
is focused on *reality*. Peter Drucker, writer and corporate guru in leadership, claims that the first task of any leader is to define reality (Drucker
1986). Defining reality is a dynamic process that—for the visionary
leader—encompasses head, soul, and body. Once reality is known in the
total being, it becomes the basis for all perceptions and decisions related
to the visionary call. Visionary leaders—whether they are political, social, or religious—use this experienced reality to discipline their call.
They do not assume responsibility for transforming all reality, but they
seek to transform the particular reality that laid claim to their total being.

The "call" for visionary leaders usually begins with a working and
experiential knowledge of an immediate situation. Often these transformative leaders have had a powerful, passionate, personal encounter with
some social oppression. From this experience they have more than an
intellectual working knowledge of a social reality; they also have a personal feeling relating to that condition. Passion and knowledge combine
to inform a new substantial reality. Here is the difference between management and visionary leadership. The visionary leader has the capacity
to see another reality beyond what is immediately visible. Such a vision
emerges from a time of incubation after the encounter, and once a vision
emerges, it becomes the foundation and motivation of visionary leadership.

Significant contemporary literature on leadership underscores the
importance of vision to accomplishing mission. The economic and

corporate world now actively uses the language of *vision* and *mission*—
terms that were once the sole (soul) possession of the religious community. Additionally, the corporate world provides numerous workshops
and events designed to stimulate and nurture one's imagination and visionary capacity. But what of the local congregation with its emphasis
on continuity and tradition? In this generation of traditionalists and tech-
nocrats, managers and problem solvers who sustain the status quo, does
the church see itself as fertile ground for vision and visionary leadership?

A commitment to community ministries provides a breeding ground
for visionary leadership. Encountering the community offers the context
for holy discontent. Holy discontent provides the genius for vision, and
vision gives authority to religious and social visionary leadership.
Individuals in congregations who allow their passions to be moved by
the realities of social community are a natural source for the inspiration
of vision within the congregation. In this sense the community serves
the congregation. The discovery, acknowledgment, and nurture of a
sense of "holy discontent" with some aspect of this social reality are the
genius of vision and of visionary leaders.

The nurturing ingredient for such vision is imagination. Although
imagination is a universal capacity, it is often inaccessible because it has
been unnurtured and underdeveloped. Nurture and development come
through practice.

Lewis Carroll in *Through the Looking Glass* had a humorous yet
insightful perspective on this natural but often unnurtured capacity:

> "Let's consider your age. To begin with, how old are you?"
> "I am seven and a half exactly."
> "You needn't say exactly," the queen remarked, "I can believe it
> without that. Now I'll give you something to believe. I am just one
> hundred and one, four months and a day."
> "I can't believe that," said Alice.
> "Can't you?" the queen said in a pitying tone. "Try again. Draw
> a long breath and shut your eyes."
> Alice laughed. "There's no use trying," she said, "one can't be-
> lieve impossible things."
> "I dare say you haven't had much practice," said the queen,
> "when I was your age I always did it for half an hour a day. Why
> sometimes I believed as many as six impossible things before
> breakfast." (Carroll 1988)

Holy Discontent

The ability to believe the impossible is essential for visionary leaders. As long as church members are content with defining reality by only what seems possible, they are locked into a rather objective and often sterile world. Holy discontent is often the force that breaks the imprisonment of the imagination and enables individuals, congregations, and communities to see new realities.

When holy discontent occurs in a church, great energy is released in one of two directions—resistance or response. Either the congregation resists the opportunity, or the members address the conditions that cause the discontent. If holy discontent is experienced in the vision that emerges and the church dismisses the vision, then it may diminish or even end the life of the church. If, through experiencing a social reality in a community, holy discontent is experienced and the congregation responds to the emerging vision, it often furthers the life and health of the church. Acknowledging the significance and implication for churches when they face social realities that cause holy discontent strongly suggests congregations take the relationship with their communities seriously.

The visionary leader who experiences holy discontent and allows the passions to free the imagination is free to see a new reality. This new reality, however, may not be easily visible to others. At this point the visionary leader becomes an artist. The visionary leader first will communicate that there is another reality, and then will artistically find ways to give pictures of that new vision.

Establishing images of an alternative reality is the initial work of the visionary leader who has assumed responsibility for changing reality. This is not always easy. The alternative reality is, after all, something unseen and unknown and therefore difficult to believe. Drama seems to be the most frequently used and the most effective means to create images of new possibilities. Frequently, visionary leaders are storytellers, and they are often individuals around whom stories accumulate.

Using Stories

We know that people are moved to change their ideas, attitudes, and behaviors through symbolic stories. Mental and attitudinal transformation seldom occurs as a result of viewing pie charts, bar graphs, or three-inch statistical appendices to three-hundred-page reports. In a different kind of research, Joanne Martin of Stanford University worked with MBA students to discover what type of communication was most effective in convincing people about an unseen reality (Martin and Paivers 1982). In attempting to convince a number of MBA students regarding the sincerity of a particular firm's policy of avoiding layoffs, she divided the students into three separate groups. She presented one group with an illustrated story. Another group received a wealth of statistical evidence indicating the firm had far less involuntary turnover than normal for the industry. A third group got both the story and the stats. The most convinced group received only the story.

Most of us openly acknowledge that the power of religious faith lies not in dogma, but in story. Stories open options and energize people to do new things they previously had not imagined or sometimes even resisted. The best leaders in all fields, especially in chaotic conditions, are master artists of symbols, often storytellers. Martin Luther King, Jr., called this creating a "sense of drama."

In the Church and Community Project one of the most powerful stories emerged from the conflict between volunteers in the Mustard Seed Ministry and some doctors providing medical care in an Indiana town. As the director tells the story, a single mother on welfare took her child with a high fever to a doctor's office about closing time. They were abruptly denied care, and the receptionist told them that "your green card [for state-supported medical care] won't help you here, or anywhere in this town." Although the child found medical care in another town the next day, the volunteer from the Mustard Seed was shocked. She refused to be satisfied by the receptionist's and later the doctor's explanation that the woman could have been treated free—but the green card required too much paperwork. She refused to be pacified by other medical personnel who said that the child was not in danger, and the doctor's office had followed "established medical practice."

The volunteer told the story of that single mother and her sick child until the churches of the community requested a public meeting of all the doctors in town to explain their procedures and reassure a doubting community that emergency medical care would be available for all who needed it. It was a stormy meeting. Several well-known doctors let it be known that they felt maligned by a nosy volunteer who did not understand the complexity of medical records, and the volunteer with her associates kept elaborating on their story and demanding new, more creative answers from the medical establishment. In the meeting everyone made concessions, and a new procedure for indigent care emerged. Green cards are no longer a barrier to medical attention because one visionary volunteer had a story and told it well.

Throughout history, stories stir action. "Once upon a time in a land far beyond the mountains,,." has tremendous power to initiate changed perceptions, attitudes, and behaviors. The visionary leader, aware of the preciousness of the acquired vision, intuitively knows not to trust the vision to the realm of reason and rational thought where it can be slaughtered and abused by analysis and critique. Additionally, the visionary leader intuitively knows that the only place for the treasured vision is in the realm of passions, which are both accessed and protected by and through the imagination.

When a congregation is free to push deeply into the collective imagination and tell stories out of its collective imagination as well as out of its history, establishing connections and building mythologies that have universal acknowledgment and application become easier. Such connections with the larger world certainly have implications for the community in which the congregation exists. The congregation that permits itself to both recognize and create legends and myths travels beneath the surface of immediate reality to an unusual place of depth where spirit and life abide.

Visionary leaders realize that not only is story the carrier of history and tradition, story is also a timeless source of energy for social transformation. Once allowed to tell their stories, visionary leaders become both containers and dispensers of power. One cannot consider aspects of visionary leadership within a congregation without addressing the multidimensional aspects of such power. In an observational research project that was designed to identify the dimensions of leadership for those in urban ministry, I discovered upon review of the interviews that the questions, dynamics, and issues of power were always raised by the interviewee. The dynamics of power seem to be always present when there are active visionary leaders. Experienced, transformative leaders are seldom naive to the realities of their power.

Sharing Power and Vision

Transformative, visionary leaders often acknowledge and are comfortable with their own power. They talk with satisfaction about accessing that power, and they are comfortable being in acknowledged positions of power. In addition, they seem to experience little shame. This lack of personal shame contributes to their acceptance of others in positions of power without jealousy or threat. Repeatedly, I have discovered that transformative leaders enjoy confrontation with "powers and principalities," and they further enjoy telling stories of such confrontation—even when they lost. They believe that such conflict tested and brought out the best in them and in the people with whom they were working.

That visionary leaders comfort with power is significant because it stands in contrast to the often repeated dictum of Lord Acton, "Power corrupts." For visionary leaders, their comfort with power inflates their capacity to empower others. There is a positive correlation between an individual's comfort with his or her own power and the ability to empower others.

In the Church and Community Project, the Rev. Larry Trotter is a large man with a commanding presence who has a background in Gospel music and a flare for the dramatic. As pastor of Sweet Holy Spirit Church on the south side in Chicago, he leads worship with a great choir of singers and hundreds of worshippers in each of several Sunday services. Although others might be content with the activities within the sanctuary, Larry regularly walks the streets of his community with several hundred of his followers, singing with them and preaching the gospel of love in the very places where drugs are sold, prostitutes are in evidence, families are broken, and children wander without parental attention. His voice, his beliefs, and his invitations empower others to face the brutal realities of their community, and in the shelter of his powerful presence, some change their lives and join the community of believers that he represents.

Not everyone is a Larry Trotter, but there is truth in the often repeated definition, a leader is someone who has followers. While that definition itself is simplistic, it points to the necessity to move ownership of the vision from the dreamer to the followers. Empowerment comes through ownership. The degree to which visionary leaders are able to transfer ownership of the vision is a measure of their capacity to empower others. This, too, is an art.

Power, especially in social and political settings, is a resource that can be used by both leaders and followers who are stirred by holy discontent and who share vision that emerges from this holy discontent. Such power is the opposite of paternalism and patronizing that unfortunately may be employed in the name of empowerment. Visionary leaders attract followers who are often unreasonably loyal. Together such leaders and followers create a dynamic and a force that may be disturbing for an administrative leader who inflates the importance of maintaining control.

Holy discontent involves passion. Because passionate leaders have assessed the capacity to see a reality beyond what is immediately visible, there is an added unmeasurable dimension of power that, when shared, empowers the community and creates passionate followers. Unfortunately, encountering such power often strikes fear in the hearts of those who embrace the importance of maintaining the status quo.

Community of Vision

To put it bluntly, visionary leaders are often troublemakers. Instead of obeying and following the expressed lines of constituted authority, they frequently are driven, and they pursue their unseen reality through whatever channel works. The troublemaking quickly multiplies when the vision is shared by others either in the congregation or in the community, or in both. Congregations make judgments, either consciously or unconsciously, about their intimacy with community based on their perceived ability to function out of a degree of chaos. Three options or levels of congregational/community intimacy suggest the range of possibilities for the congregation:

1. The congregation gets close enough to *serve* the community.
2. The congregation gets close enough to *partner* with the community.
3. The congregation gets close enough to *unite* with the community.

The service motif is by far the most common for congregations. The service industry is now the fastest-growing industry in the United States, and the service motif is very American. Everyone from McDonald's to Macintosh wants to serve us to market services. The church, while not selling a service product, may choose the service motif based on a theology of servanthood. A quick review of the recent flood of written materials on leadership reflects that one of the most dominant themes is servant leadership. This theme is strong in the corporate and the not-for-profit worlds.

Partnership is also a popular motif. This motif, while allowing for differences, focuses on a common, if not higher, objective for all. It allows for independence and calls for commitment not to a partnership, but the goals and objectives to be achieved through partnership. Often such partnerships move into developing deeper, more committed relationships between the congregation and the community.

Uniting with communities remains the most difficult motif for congregations to envision. This motif dramatically challenges congregational identity. It raises questions about a church's historic theology and invites a dialogue with ideas and values that do not originate from the congregation. Uniting with the community presses the church beyond servant and partner modes, and invites the church to stand with the oppressed when that community needs voice and strength.

Historically, congregations have grown and moved with their social communities. They were legitimate institutions because they shared the fate of their community. In the United States such a relationship between church and community has declined significantly with a resulting acceptance of separation of church and community. Legitimacy now seems to hover more around either doctrine or worship style than relationships to a context or community.

Shared vision around a social agenda has a remarkable potential to unite congregations and communities. When vision is compelling enough to be a force in people's hearts both in the larger social community and in the congregation, it becomes a common ground for communication. Communication is the backbone of relationships.

When individuals have a similar image of an invisible reality and are committed to that picture, they often become committed to one another. This commitment energizes a relationship between a congregation and a community through the shared vision. When people share a vision, they are connected, bound together through a common aspiration. Just as personal vision generates power for the individual, shared vision generates power for the collective.

The pastor of Edwin Ray Memorial United Methodist Church, as reflected in one published report on the Church and Community Project, embodies the visionary leader who gives and gains strength from the community she serves.

> Pastor Mattie not only lives her faith, she helps her members articulate the faith they are living with her. They have, in her words, gained confidence that God can use them in the things they are already doing, and more. She calls it "experiencing the wholeness of word and deed." She calls them Gideon's army. (Dudley and Johnson 1993)

Peter Senge in his book *The Fifth Discipline* illustrates the power of the common sharing of vision and the resulting commitment by referring to the movie *Spartacus*, which is an adaptation of the story of a Roman gladiator/slave who led an army of slaves in an uprising in 71 B.C. (Senge 1990). This army of slaves defeated the Roman legions twice, but was finally overpowered by the general Marcus Crassus after a long siege and battle. In the movie General Crassus told the thousand survivors in Spartacus's army, "You have been slaves, you will be slaves again, but you will be spared your rightful punishment of death by the mercy of the Roman Empire. All you need to do is turn over to me the slave Spartacus because we do not know him by sight."

After a long pause, Spartacus stood up, announcing, "I am Spartacus." Then the man next to him also stood, saying, "I am Spartacus." As the spirit seized the group, the next man shouted, "No, I am Spartacus." Within a minute everyone in the army was standing.

Whether the story is apocryphal or not, it demonstrates a deep truth. By standing up, each man chose death. Senge suggests that the loyalty of Spartacus's army was not to Spartacus the man, but their loyalty was to a shared vision, a vision in which they could see themselves as free men—a vision that Spartacus had inspired. The vision was so compelling that no man could bear to give it up and return to slavery.

Challenge

The opportunity to free such visionary leaders in the church begins by
listening for the imaginative stories being told in the congregation and
identifying both the storytellers and the individuals around whom these
stories develop. Not only is this an essential and enjoyable starting
place, it is also a process that produces new life. It requires intentional
sensitivity and attention to the stirring of dreams and stories generated
from community context.

Visions are exhilarating. They create the spark that lifts a congregation out of the mundane. They create ownership and pride because
shared vision changes people's relationships with each other and with the
church. The congregation becomes "our church." A shared vision is the
first step in allowing people who mistrusted each other to begin working
together. Shared visions compel courage so naturally that members of
the congregation begin living by faith without being asked to do so. This
courage simply means doing whatever is needed in pursuit of the vision.
Shared vision fosters risk taking and experimentation, which are natural
behaviors and responses when a congregation unites with its community.

A shared vision that is intrinsic to the congregation and its immediate community uplifts and energizes the congregation's aspirations.
Ministry becomes part of pursuing a larger purpose embodied in the
congregation's shared vision. This sense of mission is reflected in the
congregation's style, climate, and spirit.

PART 2

Organization

CHAPTER 4

Organizing for Social Ministry

Carl S. Dudley

"Sir, you're messing with my hierarchy," intoned a large male African-American pastor. He was explaining his dissent as we described our organizational guidelines for developing church-based social ministries in the Church and Community Project. When we announced our expectation that a layperson in each church would chair the local ministry committee, the pastor responded that, in his black Baptist tradition, the clergy are in charge.

Formal or Familial Organizing Style?

In organizing to support community ministries, we found that congregations typically assume one or the other of two familiar organizational styles. Either they articulate a formal style, or they naturally assume a familial informal style. In this chapter we build on these alternate types of organization. Although these two styles are easily recognized, we rarely found them in a pure form. Rather, they were shaped by situational factors in each setting. We will first introduce the dichotomy and then consider variations.

About half of the congregations were managerial oriented and task centered. True to form, in developing social ministries they began to build a *formal organization.* They identified officers, clear goals, specific responsibilities, subcommittees with assignments, and job descriptions for personnel. They operated with reports, formal motions, votes for decisions, and Robert's Rules of Order. Board members were selected for specific contributions of skills and resources. Frequently, they began with an adoption of a statement of purpose and bylaws, often followed by a move toward separate incorporation.

The other half of the planning committees were more relational. Since they did business more like a family, we called their style a *familial organization*. For board vacancies they found friends who were also well known and trusted in the community, and together they did what needed to get done. Like the formal organization, they reported officers and committee chairs; but typically, their reported responsibilities did not reflect the tasks each person did. They made decisions by consensus, kept essential records but no formal minutes, assigned duties to the most willing person, and added new board members as they needed help in the same way that they had first joined—by asking the people they knew would fit in. They intuitively believed that commitment and affection would compensate for whatever people lacked in expertise.

Both styles worked, with differing effectiveness. The formal style was easier to track but slower to act. Sometimes the formal organizations seemed on the verge of talking the project to death, as if they preferred discussion to action. The familial groups consistently moved more swiftly, with a larger percentage of the available people involved. But they sometimes got in trouble with their records, were harder for partners to join, and often had a difficult time finding new members for the initial team. Each style had advantages and liabilities, and the leaders who were most effective used a programmatic combination of both organizational dynamics.

Complex Patterns from Simple Themes

Once we had identified the formal and familial approaches to organizing ministries, we could better understand the wide variations we found in Church and Community Ministries. First, of course, we never found pure types. In all the ministries we found times when they focused and organized their actions, and in all we noted the foundational activity of human bonding. Thus, although churches tended to emphasize one style over another, in practice every project included elements of both: The most task-centered boards often operated informally and included close personal friends, and the most relational core committees had moments of managerial efficiency, as if to prove they could do it when they needed to. This combination of styles had double implications. At times each style incorporated elements of the other to become a mixture of both. But there were limits to their inclusiveness—under sustained pressure or in a sudden crisis, each tended to snap back to the original approach, like a rubber band that has been stretched too far.

More important, the congregation's situation seemed to shape its primary organizational decisions, as seen in the lens of *formal* and *familial* organizational styles. For leaders who sought to use the natural energy of congregations in particular situations, we found that organizational patterns were strongly affected by several historical and contextual factors:

- congregational size
- community location
- cultural orientation
- cross-cultural ministry
- faith-driven ministry
- dysfunctional community
- time frame for change

1. Small Churches: They have a similar style, but location makes a difference.

Initially, small and large churches seem to follow an anticipated script. Small churches tend toward familial patterns while large churches develop more formal boards.

In particular, small urban and town churches are especially swift in mobilizing programs with broader support than the slower, more complex development of a formal organizational structure. These churches can inform their members more rapidly, receive members' support more quickly, and initially act more swiftly. With a leadership mixture of group consensus and individual trust they can move almost immediately into new ministries. For example, in one town a coalition of small churches decided to work on housing rehabilitation, purchased the house, and mobilized the volunteers long before their organization had developed its working style. Among friends, they did what needed doing. As these ministries mature, they evolve into collegial combinations but retain much of their informal style.

Small rural churches follow the familial patterns, but at a different pace. Although some of the larger rural churches may appear to have a formal organization, they still operate like a family—for example, friends are committee members, decisions are reached by consensus, people accept responsibilities regardless of their job titles. But rural churches take longer to reach decisions than comparable urban congregations. When asked, members of rural and small town churches say that they take their time because they live inescapably in the same community and they need to get along. Others point out that the pace of life is simply slower. "Time in a small town," as one pastor explained, "is not measured in hours and minutes, but in milestones and landmarks."

Further, rural church groups are more aware of the absence of resources that unify and give identity in their fractured communities. As compared with other settings, rural churches develop inclusive programs with more investment in capital assets than program staff. Half of our rural/small town ministries raised substantial funding that, along with project seed money, they used to construct facilities for use by the whole community. Urban congregations of similar size, by contrast, focused on the problems of particular populations, such as a center for teenagers or a shelter for battered women. Perhaps for that reason, rural ministry boards reflect community-wide representation, while urban ministries are guided by people with more specialized interests.

2. Larger Churches: Denomination makes a difference.

Larger churches take time to develop more formal organizations, which can become immersed in their own procedures. Protestant and Catholic churches treat this differently.

Typically, large Protestant churches become so engaged in process that decision making preempts program. For example, when a Presbyterian church of middle management families called in two experts who strongly disagreed, the committee argued for months between the merits of the two positions. In a large Methodist church the organizing committee decided that they should not define their program until they had hired their professional staff, but they could not hire their staff without some decisions about program; finally, they hired the staff first, and with their help decided on their program.

In metropolitan Catholic churches ministry projects are designed and developed by a relatively new form of religious professional called the parish associate. With the decline among available priests, Catholic parishes are turning to nuns and lay associates to guide parish programs. In these situations the lines of authority are often unclear. In developing ministries in our project, the parish associates were eventually caught between the value judgments of the priest and the program ambitions of the lay ministry board; in each case the priest prevailed or the ministry departed. Catholic parishes may develop a collegial style, but in the crunch "Father" is still responsible and in charge. The Catholic parish was organizationally a family church.

3. Organizational styles reflect ethnic traditions.

The African-American pastor in a black church remains the pivotal figure at the center of congregational life. Although the pastor may check quietly with key individuals before announcing decisions, in the eyes of the congregation, every church activity requires the pastor's blessing. In trust and love, they vest their pastor with the authority to make decisions, and they support those decisions as firmly as if the whole congregation had taken a vote.

We find a similar if less pronounced pattern of hierarchical empowerment among both Hispanic and Asian churches. They use a combination of a formal organization, a familial process, and a pastor who remains the pivotal person in congregational decisions. When the pastor of Sweet Holy Spirit Baptist Church saw a threat to his "hierarchy" (above), he reflected the authority that many ethnic, racial, and immigrant congregations place in the office and person of the pastor. In our experience ethnic churches were traditionally (not organizationally) family churches.

4. In cross-cultural ministries, there is a clash in organizational styles.

Cross-cultural ministries are naturally in tension between formal and familial organizational styles—it comes with the territory. Typically, Euro-American leaders assume a formal, democratic organizational style, and leaders from the other cultures—Asian, Hispanic, and African-American—assume a more familial style with the pastor as pivotal figure, the father of the family. The Anglo style pushes for planning, group decisions, reports, and organizational efficiency, while the familial style is more informal, personal, laid-back but responsive to solve problems as needed.

In one sharp expression of cultural conflict, the Anglo leader of a cross-cultural program characterized her ministry as a "missionary situation" where the immigrant culture was "unprepared to cope with this new life." The solution for this leader was to manage their ministry for them while they "learned our ways." In most situations leaders on both sides transcended the differences through their understanding, appreciation, and empathy. But these cultural differences remain, to be endured and understood without being easily, or perhaps ever, resolved.

Similar cross-cultural tensions exist in other ministries. Cultural gaps are evident between wealth and poverty, between strict religious beliefs and cultural accommodation, between people of different perceptions and experiences. In the ministry program for and by people who are deaf, sharp cultural conflict occurred between the members who are hearing impaired and, as they said, the majority who are "sign impaired" (unskilled in American Sign Language). Like racial and ethnic groups, hearing impaired people have a cultural identity of their own, but in that culture they have little experience in formal organizational procedures. From the problems in translation, unfamiliarity with the process, and a fun-loving disdain toward organizational decisions, board meetings are long and decisions difficult. As board members enact their skills and frustrations, meetings become a kind of stage where continuing tensions of cultural conflict are enacted in slow motion, sometimes with mutually rewarding results.

5. In cross-cultural ministries, bridge people are essential.

Beyond the differences in formal and familial organizational styles, in cross-cultural social ministries, we discover an array of unique people who perform an essential function almost unobserved. In every successful cross-cultural ministry, we find a translator or bridge person (or group) for continual negotiation and interpretation between the outside society and the inside culture of a particular group.

In a black Baptist church the project treasurer negotiated between the familial style of the congregation and the formal expectations of the funding agency. In a combination of a university parish and a blue-collar church, the gap was bridged by a parish associate who worked in one and lived in the other parish. In a white church working to reach an African-American community, the bridge person was Anglo in origin, but ordained by the AME Church. In the overheated feelings of a small town against its pacifist minority, the bridge was made by an ex-GI reformed alcoholic who discovered in his suffering the importance of reconciliation.

In every successful cross-cultural project we find an unrecognized saint, a bicultural person who bridges the gap to interpret each to the other while the ministry is developing its own cohesive identity. Bridge people appear in both formal and informal organizational styles, with and without official status, and generally unrecognized but always important.

6. Vision-driven ministries have distinctive leadership styles.

A distinct leadership style guides ministries that have strong, explicitly theological vision that seeks to transform the world as they find it. Although these ministries are often comfortable with many aspects of the larger society, in the specific areas that they wish to change, these are countercultural ministries.

Such countercultural ministries are found in every segment of society, in every faith group of our study. Some are born again, like the Methodists who care about community unemployment; some are frustrated by denominational shortsightedness, like the mainline Presbyterians who share a building with three other community agencies; some want the kingdom of God to transform substandard housing in the inner city. In Chicago one African-American Pentecostal pastor leads demonstrators in the streets against the drug use in his community, with hundreds of his followers singing hymns and shouting, "Death to drugs! Come to the Light." In Lafayette an equally determined but soft-spoken group challenges the inadequacies of the courts, and offers an alternative agency for victim-offender reconciliation. In the energy of their commitments they transcend more typical organizational styles.

Vision-driven ministries combine the formal and familial styles, but the mix is not collegial in the usual sense. Rather, they feel driven by the Spirit as envisioned by uniquely articulate and gifted leaders. In the fray their leaders are strong, their members are committed, and their organizations are united more by purpose than by structure.

7. Sometimes dysfunctional leaders seem essential.

Some communities are overwhelmed by problems that are insoluble for the people who live there. There is no ready solution for structural unemployment, family disintegration, inadequate schools, teen pregnancy, or isolated elderly people who live in poverty. Surviving at a subsistence level, some groups make do with whatever is available and make no false claims about personal success or social transformation. From an outsider's perspective, since they are not solving problems they may be branded as dysfunctional groups with equally dysfunctional leaders. Such ministries often lack either familial or formal organizational foundations—they just limp along.

Although these groups may not expect to effect great changes, they remain where others have departed, and they give comfort in communities that are tormented by addictions and betrayed by false hopes. Theologically, these groups talk of a faith that sustains them, but unlike the vision-driven ministries, they have no illusions about having a decisive impact. Sustained by God, they support others. In response to appeals to get his ministry more focused, one pastor among our congregations explained that "dysfunctional groups are appropriate for dysfunctional communities—it's meeting people where they are."

8. Time expectations shape decision-making styles.

A sense of time also affected the organizational style of ministry. We have already noted the slower pace in rural communities that sustains a relaxed and unrushed decision-making schedule among most rural ministries.

In a similar way, a sense of God's time shapes the organization in other congregations. In Sweet Holy Spirit Baptist Church, where the phrase "God will provide" is heard frequently, members live in the present, and they denote such organizational exercises as planning, budgeting, and fund-raising as an absence of faith in God's constant care. By contrast, the professionals who mobilized the ministries of several managerial congregations seemed more alive when they were planning the next step into the future of their project, and they disdained as almost less than real the boring maintenance of daily program. But the longest time frame for planning came in the group that developed the Center for Conflict Resolution. With an extended history of persecution for their pacifist stands, these Anabaptist believers were willing to invest in the next generation of children and youth with the confidence that the young people may change what their forebears could not.

Although it did not change the mix of formal and familial organizational styles, the theological-cultural sense of timing strongly influenced the energy and urgency that leaders invested in making their organizations productive.

We Advocate Theological Pragmatism

We know that both formal and familial organizational styles can be effective, especially when supported by an appreciative pastor. When we found significant tension within and between projects based on organizational expectations, we looked for the styles that seemed appropriate for each setting. By honoring the indigenous organizational style(s), church leaders may reduce inappropriate expectations and at the same time harness the natural energy of a community to build community ministries. Among our ministries we found the following patterns:

1. Small churches, which tend to be more familial, move more rapidly toward decision in urban areas, more slowly in rural communities.

2. Among large churches, which tend toward formal organizations, Protestants are often tangled in procedure, while Catholics develop formal structures with familylike styles, organized by parish associates, but ultimately guided by the priest.

3. In African-American, Asian, and Hispanic churches, where organizations may look formal but act familial, the pastor remains the pivotal figure.

4. Cross-cultural ministries frequently reflect tension between the formal and familial organizational styles. Bridge people, often quiet saints, appear to make possible these ministries.

5. Vision-driven ministries, with their strong leadership, transcend formal and familial in the energy of their commitments.

6. Dysfunctional communities may have programs to match without either formal or familial styles, but simply survive in chaos.

7. Congregations carry a theological-cultural sense of time that shapes the urgency and energy of their commitments.

With this much diversity in organizational styles, we advocate theological pragmatism: the "dogmatic assertion" to hang loose until you find the ways to organize that match the needs and values of participants. Theological pragmatism does not import alien expectations. Rather, work hard, learn from the situation, and make the most of whatever happens. Although the goals of ministry are universal, the organizational process must fit each group in its own setting.

CHAPTER 5

Social Ministries: Constructive Use of Community Tensions

Carl S. Dudley and Susan E. Sporte

Introduction

The Christian Service Program (CSP) in Canton, Illinois, assists seniors
in completing their Medicare and health insurance forms, offers volunteer income tax assistance, and meets similar simple clerical needs.
When asked what they are doing "to advocate justice for marginalized
peoples," the part-time staff and personable volunteers laugh at the idea
of changing the world. They jokingly call advocacy the "A word" and
strongly deny any interest in controversy. By intentionally inserting
"Service" in the middle of the name, CSP emphasized caring for individuals rather than changing systems. Social justice is not the chosen
priority.

But when these gentle souls discovered that the county ambulance
service in Canton was being curtailed, they led the charge for a new
ambulance service to take its place. When they found that some insurance companies were ignoring or hassling their clients, they forced the
companies to take special care of the senior citizens from Canton. And
when they realized that one of the many forms for the Social Security
Administration made no sense, they leaned on the agency until Social
Security changed its form! Like the majority of the Church and Community Ministries, they did not try to develop advocacy programs—but it
happened naturally.

Typical churches can develop both service ministries that touch the
lives of individuals and justice ministries that advocate changes in
dysfunctional systems and agencies. Service programs are relatively
easy to organize in most situations. But in developing intentional

programs of advocacy, most churches feel either that the task is inappropriate or that they have failed in performance. Yet looking back, we
discover that the majority of our church-based social ministries have
precipitated systemic changes in their communities.

You can combine service and justice ministries in three ways:

1. *Extension of ministry*: Every congregation can engage in a ministry
of service and justice when it builds on the strengths of its ordinary,
ongoing ministry.

2. *Modeling ministry*: Many congregations can begin new ministries
when they see them modeled by others, and many existing ministries can
change their communities by modeling alternative procedures that are
adopted by established social agencies.

3. *Confrontational ministry*: At the right moment with careful preparation, confrontational challenges can change the oppressive programs,
policies, and personnel of existing community social conditions.

Each approach surprised us in a different way: the first by its in-
timate connection with the faith roots of congregational strength; the
second by its simplicity and unanticipated impact; and the third by its
highly focused effectiveness.

Background

The typical programs that developed through the Center for Church and
Community Ministries reach many community groups, such as preschool
children and teen parents, latchkey rural kids and city kids on the streets,
adult literacy and crisis counseling, home repairs and transitional housing, elderly people in their homes and in community settings, neighborhood improvement and community development. To develop these
ministries, congregations (1) studied their communities, (2) celebrated
their congregational identity, and (3) developed a supportive organization to implement their decisions (as described in *Basic Steps*, 1991).
These three elements are interdependent. Specifically, in studying their
communities, church leaders could not "see" conditions that they did not
believe they could change. Once they organized to develop a ministry,

they found the confidence that allowed them to recognize community issues.

In short, we found that you can rarely organize community ministries simply in response to obvious problems. Like others, your church is inflicted with "familiarity blindness" that permits passivity, ignorance, or repression of awareness. Such a condition will not heal until you get a small and committed group that believe, "by God," they are called to make a difference.

Once organized, you will discover that you have unconsciously "known" about community problems, yet been unable to admit it until you are organized for ministry. With these new eyes, you can become more personally acquainted with the community people and their problems. With that sensitivity you can reorganize your priorities to find time and energy for sustained ministry. In reviewing these three patterns in congregational strategies, you may find one or more appropriate for your situation.

1. Extension of Ministry

Every congregation can engage in social ministry when it builds on the strengths of its ordinary, ongoing ministry.

Contextual factors influence congregational attitudes toward service and justice ministries. Churches in urban areas with more highly educated members, for example, are more issue oriented and more willing to support the congregation's involvement in social causes and justice ministries. Church members in towns and rural communities are less inclined to endorse the institutional involvement of the church in controversial issues, perhaps because they place a higher premium on personal relationships.

The theological orientation of church members as liberal or conservative does not appear significant in developing social ministries. Among the congregations in the Church and Community Project, members of congregations with more evangelical views indicated as high or higher concerns for social issues, for developing social ministries, and for changing the causes of poverty. Obviously, evangelical churches cannot be categorically consigned to conservative social views, or liberal churches to liberal sociopolitical positions.

Rather, churches develop social ministries in ways that are consistent with the role they play in the community, that is, the way they define their self-image in the history of community development. We have identified five patterned self-images by the stories that churches tell about themselves in their communities (see Carl S. Dudley and Sally A. Johnson, *Energizing the Congregation* [Louisville: Westminster/John Knox, 1993]). Based on these self-images, congregations develop program, recruit members, raise funds, make decisions and, for our purposes here, develop service and justice ministries.

In developing community ministries, the five images function in this way. *Pillar churches*, as one of the basic community establishments, share a general responsibility for the good and welfare of their area. *Prophetic churches*, when they see evil, take a proactive stance to transform the condition. *Pilgrim churches* provide spiritual and cultural shelter for a sliçe of society, like national, racial, and ethnic communities. *Survivor churches* have a lifestyle of weathering crisis, and although constantly on the verge of disaster, they will endure. *Servant churches* seek to live their faith in quiet service to help particular individuals in their times of spiritual and physical need.

Your church can engage in community service and justice ministry when you build programs that are consistent with the story you live.

As a pillar church, for example, you are community teachers and civic guides. The pillar Church of the Brethren in North Manchester, for example, brought together a coalition of religious and civic leaders to establish an educational program to teach an alternative to violence in the public schools. In Kokomo, the widely respected St. Luke's United Methodist Church established the Literacy Coalition for Howard County, an agency that has been featured by the United Way as a model for community involvement in a transitional economy.

As a pillar congregation, you can use your status in a network of community institutions, when aroused, to transform your community. When particular people need help, you can employ the same networks. One pillar church pastor observed, "We do social service by telephone; we build programs and take care of people through connections."

As a prophetic congregation, you would take the opposite tack, where confrontation seems natural. In Chicago, the HANDS ministry in behalf of people who are deaf spends most of its time in service for its members (such as job placements), but it generates its most energetic support from its advocacy campaign for equal access for people who are deaf by phone to a pizza chain. In Lafayette, Shalom Church may look like other congregations in its worship, study, and fellowship, yet it solidifies its support from newspaper stories about the congregation's commitment to social justice, such as their public letters and protest marches against U.S. involvement in the Persian Gulf War.

If you are a prophetic congregation, such encounters are the way that you tell your history, and personal involvements are remembered like combat ribbons.

As a pilgrim church, you know the intense but focused boundaries of your social ministries. Such congregations are so immersed in the lives of immigrants, an ethnic group or groups, or another segment of the population that they naturally demand justice in issues that affect their own people. Sweet Holy Spirit Baptist Church will give food and clothing to any and all who come to their doors. And when they endorse candidates for public office, they ignore any distinction between the private, sacred church and the public, secular world—they are in solidarity with everything that affects the lives of their people.

As leaders in pilgrim churches, you may have felt the warmth of caring for members of a cultural family of faith. Like a family, this community may be stormy within, but it is united against the world and hostile toward any who might harm its members.

As a survivor church, you will be able to take the social ministry head-on, the same way that you treat other challenges. Like many rural communities, Washburn, Illinois, is struggling with a declining economy. Feeling trapped and pushed by circumstances beyond their control, the church leaders in the Washburn Christian Action Ministry rose up in righteous anger when faced with a threatened dump for hazardous materials. In unity they generated fierce resistance, until the dump was relocated in another community that failed to mobilize the leadership to resist.

In a survivor situation, you can find barely enough resources to tackle just one more crisis. But you can keep on that way for years.

As a servant church, you can always mobilize to help one more person. In Canton, the small community mentioned at the beginning of our chapter, the leaders of the Christian Service Program dedicated their work to helping elderly individuals deal with the blizzard of forms that they must complete. Despite their rejection of the "a" word, when

aroused they successfully challenged the county government, major insurance companies, and even the Social Security Administration. They
called this activity "only doing the essentials for the people of our town."

When your servant church becomes frustrated in the face of injustice
and enraged at abusive systems, it can move mountains.

Every church can do it when members reach out in ministry in the
way they live within the congregation. In all situations we found ample
resources for new ministries that were built on existing congregational
strengths.

2. Modeling Ministry

*Many congregations can begin new ministries when they see them
modeled by others, and many existing ministries can change their
communities by modeling alternative procedures that are adopted by
established social agencies.*

Unless you are a prophetic congregation, your members will be more
inclined to service than to justice ministries. In most churches, members
are more interested in helping individuals than changing systems. Bib-
lically, members are more likely to associate themselves with the New
Testament healing by Jesus than the Old Testament confrontations of the
prophets (although many would say that Jesus' ministry contained and
was a prophetic confrontation).

We found that many congregations gained the courage to try social
ministry when they saw it modeled in the Bible, and they discovered
examples among other congregations of their area. Social ministries are
contagious; one begets another, by example.

Typically, these were service ministries at first. Members became
theologically outspoken in their resistance to confronting oppressive
powers and principalities. They invoked the "wall of separation" between church and state, affirmed the distinction between the sacred and
the secular, and felt more comfortable with spiritual concerns in church.
For all those reasons, the advocacy for justice seemed out of sync for the
majority of typical congregations.

Yet, in reviewing the impact of the Church and Community Ministries, the majority of the programs effected significant changes in major
public institutions in their communities. They have induced this change

in their own way. They have not openly confronted, challenged, or threatened the existing structures. Rather, they created alternatives to existing systems that have been adopted and now operate as a new part of the old process.

You also can have an impact on existing systems by creating alternatives that can be incorporated and institutionalized within existing community functions. Your communities can change like these. In Bradford, a rural community of roughly two thousand people where the youth had no employment opportunities, elderly people were struggling to keep their homes repaired, and summers were a drag, the Bradford Church and Community Project found jobs for young people to maintain properties throughout the community, especially the homes of elderly people. Although the program was first conceived by church leaders, it has been integrated into the town hall for its office, and has become the second largest employer in the community—only the school system is larger.

School systems have been changed as well. In North Manchester, Indiana, a coalition of churches and community groups, led by the Church of the Brethren, created an educational reconciliation program to teach children an alternative to violence for settling their disputes. After training for both teachers and students, the program has been adopted into the curriculum and implemented on the playgrounds of the public schools. Their agency for conflict resolution has produced change in the school curriculum and procedures. More recently, it has developed contracts with local businesses and other school systems to utilize the skills in conflict resolution.

In numerous towns and cities, church-based ministries have offered alternative services that have been recognized and adopted as improvements on existing systems. In Kokomo, the Literacy Coalition for Howard County has moved from its offices in the St. Luke's United Methodist Church to public space, and it has been featured as a model agency seeking to aid their transitional economy. In Indianapolis, Partners for Westside Housing Renewal (PWHR) has been incorporated into a network for city agencies, with special expertise in the repair of owner-occupied homes. In Lafayette, the Tippecanoe Reconciliation Project offers such a preferable alternative to the present court system that it is recommended by the court and chosen by more than one hundred clients annually.

Since so much of the literature reflects only confrontational approaches to social justice, we were astonished to see how quietly yet frequently new programs transformed existing agencies simply by adoption. Modeling is the way that many churches began their social ministries, and this low-key approach seems a natural way for many congregations to change community agencies without open conflict.

You can expand your impact by modeling systemic change in an endless variety of situations. By simply doing the best you can, many congregations quietly and effectively bring change to the programs, policies, and personnel of community institutions.

3. Confrontational Ministry

At the right moment with careful preparation, confrontational challenges can change the oppressive programs, policies, and personnel of existing community social conditions.

Confrontations occurred in a variety of situations. Some advocates for change were attempting to make existing programs and agencies sensitive to populations that had been ignored or marginalized. In Chicago, the HANDS ministry seeks jobs and resources to improve the quality of life for its members who are deaf and hearing impaired. Its primary energy in advocacy is spent encouraging public agencies, like police, bus lines, television stations, and hospitals, to install equipment and train their personnel to be sensitive to the needs of hearing impaired people. Such advocacy helps these significant agencies and organizations become more sensitive to serve specific marginalized groups in the larger society.

You can have unique impact in moments of public policy debate, such as elections. Some church-based community ministries become engaged in campaigns for values they hold and even candidates who support their views. Theological and cultural differences dictate the issues they choose. In a recent school board election, a Baptist church on the south side of Chicago selected local candidates who were introduced, endorsed, and promised the support of hundreds of members during Sunday worship. In the shadow of a major university, a justice congregation in a college town marched as a natural expression of their advocacy to influence public policy. Each did it in its own way, and neither would have done what the other did.

You can develop a public expression of advocacy when concerned people become aroused at conditions they believe are unjust. When the pillar church in Tipton, Indiana, discovered that the ill child of a welfare mother whom they were counseling was not treated by a local physician, they called a meeting of church people and doctors—to talk about health care for welfare families. Their advocacy was naive and unplanned, and the meeting turned hot and stormy. Some church leaders wanted better care for welfare families, and some physicians resented public intrusion into the technical aspects of professional practices. In the end they revised community health care procedures, and participants became more sensitive to the viewpoints of others. But some tender feelings, and even unresolved tensions, linger.

You can even find advocacy ministry against sponsoring institutions when the client-member is aroused. In Springfield, Illinois, the Hope Presbyterian Church expanded its facilities to incorporate agencies of service to children, families, and elderly people. When banks and church guidelines for construction loans did not allow for such a mixture of building use, church leaders launched a campaign to change the policies of lending agencies to encourage, not discourage, such a comprehensive, seven-days-a-week ministry of the church. In its justice ministry the local church determined to change the lending policies of its national denomination.

You can rarely engage in service and justice without transforming those who seek change in others. Westminster Presbyterian Church in Peoria, Illinois, for example, launched a ministry intended to push the Peoria public schools to develop programs for teen mothers. As the school system responded the church's ministry has become responsible for transportation of the teen mothers and their children to separate programs. Out of the advocacy the agency became immersed in essential service to sustain its initial proposal. Service and justice seem natural allies and mutually supporting sources of energy.

You can find advocacy for justice as part of almost every sensitive service ministry, natural partners in more extensive congregational programs of community concern and membership support. Even in the midst of a campaign, your advocacy is sustained by networks of mutual support and spiritual sensitivity.

Leadership for Justice Ministries

If you would see up close the problems and needs of your communities,
you need active social ministries where members can become personally
involved. Two phases are intertwined. First, to generate interest, you
must talk about particular people in your community. Then, to launch
justice ministries, you must help members to see their individual concerns are part of larger, system issues.

At significant, focused moments, you can use direct confrontational
advocacy to change dysfunctional systems. Most church-initiated changes
occurred not by confrontation, but by the creation of more desirable alternatives.

Your congregations, like others, can engage in service and justice
ministries when leaders build programs that are consistent with their
congregational identities. In our interviews with active volunteers we
heard repeatedly, "Until you asked, I didn't know how much we needed
to become involved; thanks for the experience."

CHAPTER 6

Developing Effective Congregational-Based Advocacy Ministries

Kimberly Bobo and Phil Tom

In the Church and Community Project we had the opportunity to work with thirty-two Illinois and Indiana congregations in developing their advocacy ministries. We were routinely surprised at the difficulty congregations had in approaching advocacy. This chapter looks at why congregations shy away from advocacy, the paths congregations took to advocacy, and how one can help a congregation move toward advocacy.

First, some definitions. By advocacy ministries, we mean ministries that seek systemic solutions to problems, not simply individual solutions. For example, if all the children in a community are having trouble reading, there are many ways to help. Many churches set up tutoring programs. This is a fine thing to do but does not address in any systemic fashion the failure of the school system. Most tutoring programs will help twenty or thirty students, usually a small percentage of those falling through the cracks in a public school system. An advocacy approach might involve parents and concerned residents in advocating for (speaking up for) changes in the school program to ensure that all children learn to read. Although both tutoring and working to reform school systems are important things to do, many more congregations will establish tutoring programs than will get involved in school reform. Advocacy is using love plus power to seek justice in society.

Why Congregations Shy Away from Advocacy

Our experience with congregations indicates that congregations shy away from advocacy for at least five reasons.

First, when congregations consider doing community ministries, they think in terms of serving groups of people. All the congregations in the Church and Community Project were asked to develop a community ministry in one of six problem areas: health, employment, housing, education, hunger, or world peace. Many of these churches could not or would not define their advocacy ministry in terms of any of these problem areas. They preferred to develop their ministry in terms of the people they wanted to serve, such as the people down in the valley or the seniors living in the housing project or the youth in their community.

The Kaleidoscope Project, for example, decided to work with the young people in the community since many school dropouts were hanging out in the streets with little to do. When we tried to get this project to focus on developing either an employment or an educational program with the youth, the project leaders resisted a focus because they wanted to be holistic in their service with the youth. Like many of the Church and Community Ministry Projects, the Kaleidoscope Project concentrated on a particular group in their community rather than issues or problem areas.

We found that when a congregation focuses on the person rather than on the issue, it frequently ignores the societal problems that are impacting the persons it seeks to serve, at least initially. We had this experience with one project where the congregation and its partners developed a volunteer-based literacy tutoring program to nonreading adults, with a goal of improved employability. When we asked project leaders whether the project should address the local school system to ask why it was not dealing with the issue of adult literacy, the project leaders felt that structural change was not the purpose nor their responsibility.

The groups of people selected for help are usually known to members of the congregation. The concern for this ministry arises out of their love for people, but it is usually limited to approaches that "serve" these particular people. These social services may be the most direct and immediate way to address the problems. But advocacy approaches are likely to affect more people for a longer time.

Second, some congregations are out of touch with the community.

In developing their outreach ministry, some congregations will talk to their members, read and study "the issues," and then develop their advocacy ministry without ever consulting the people they seek to serve! Without their participation the ministry that the congregation develops may be paternalistic to the community it seeks to serve; even more, it may not address the issues that are impacting the lives of the people the congregation wishes to reach.

For example, one congregation wanted to develop a community center to provide a variety of services for the young people living around its church building. The congregational leaders never consulted the young people about what they wanted in the development of the youth center. The project eventually failed because the young people did not attend the center since it did not meet their needs. This is another unfortunate example of a congregation where the members seem to be more motivated by serving their own needs to help others rather than by serving the needs of the people they claimed they wanted to reach.

A third reason congregations shy away from advocacy ministries is that they do not really believe they can make a difference, especially for big problems, like hunger and unemployment. Churches often feel that it is much easier to work on charitable solutions, like creating a feeding program, than to deal with system change, such as addressing the lack of jobs or poverty wages paid by many service industry jobs. Charitable ministries enable church members to feel good about themselves because they believe they are helping keep "somebody" nourished, clothed, and housed even if it's just for one day!

A fourth reason congregations shy away from advocacy is that they are uncomfortable discussing and using power. In one vivid example the church members who worked on painting and rehabbing homes of homebound neighbors knew that many of the dilapidated homes in their communities were owned by landlords who did not care about their properties or the community. Some of the project leaders wanted to organize the congregation and members of the community to challenge the city to force the landlords to fix up their properties. But many church members did not want to get involved, saying, "Politics is not the role of the church or the church-based ministry." These Christians confuse power with evil. Dr. Martin Luther King, Jr., frequently said that power without love is dangerous, while love without power is insipid; together power and love produce justice.

A final reason congregations shy away from advocacy is a lack of recognized authority to act by the pastors and biblical ignorance about God's desire for justice. If church members know only how God's Word speaks to our individual lives, they will think in terms of ministries to individuals. But when they know how God cares for communities, they may lead more toward ministries that advocate changing systems of oppression and exploitation.

Paths to Advocacy

There are many paths to advocacy, but we observed three basic patterns.

First, community ministries that are designed by and run by the "affected" people tend to have the strongest initial advocacy components. The HANDS program, designed and run by deaf and hearing impaired people, was crafted as an advocacy ministry. If advocacy solutions seem within the range of possibility, people directly affected by problems are more willing to challenge systems and "rock the boat" than people not directly affected.

Second, many community ministries that built in strong listening/ discernment components and paid attention to what they heard found out about community problems needing advocacy responses. One congregation initially thought they could ignore neighborhood housing and economic development concerns because there was a strong community development corporation in the area.

Once members of the congregation began talking with community residents, great dissatisfaction was unearthed. Not only was there interest in looking at new programs, but residents wanted to advocate to change the existing agency. The congregation helped form an alternative, grassroots community-controlled agency and began challenging the existing agency to be more responsive to community needs. Eventually, the two agencies merged into one, and a board was created that is controlled by community residents. This congregation moved forward in an unexpected direction because of its serious listening process.

The third and perhaps most frequent way that congregations, especially primarily middle-class congregations, move to advocacy is by learning about broader problems in the process of providing services. Members of congregations may have their eyes and ears opened to experience the systems that are unjustly impacting the lives of the people they are serving. For example, one congregation in a small town that decided to provide human services for the "poor" folks in their community discovered that the folks had to go to the emergency room to be treated for routine illnesses. The doctors in the community refused to treat poor folks because their Medicaid reimbursement was not financially feasible!

This congregation could have ignored this gross act of medical malice; after all, poor people could still go to the emergency room. But in working with the folks who suffered from this system of medical neglect, members of the congregation decided to publicly question the medical community about this practice. The situation was complicated by the fact that some of the doctors were also members of the congregation whose members were publicly questioning this medical practice. The outcome was that the larger community became informed and aware of this issue, they debated the issue, and eventually, the practice was changed.

The members of this congregation probably never imagined when they started their social service ministry that they would be standing up with the people they served against some of the civic and medical leaders of their community. But when they discovered the acts of injustice that the people suffered at the hands of their fellow members and neighbors, the church members could not stand by and continue to do business as usual! Their acts of charity led them to exercise acts of justice. They underwent a conversion experience in working with their neighbors from which they had gained the courage and strength to go beyond the safe limits of charitable ministry to the analysis that led them to create a system change.

This movement toward advocacy from direct experience with people in need seems the most likely way for congregations, which are not initially receptive to advocacy, to move toward advocacy. On the other hand, some congregations never move toward advocacy.

Helping a Congregation Move to Advocacy

By observing why some congregations shy away from advocacy and others choose this difficult ministry, we offer the following guidelines for helping a congregation develop prophetic commitment to advocate essential systemic change.

1. Seek to involve people directly affected by problems in the design and implementation of community ministries. As was indicated above, projects designed by and implemented by people affected by problems tend to be the ones that move most quickly to advocacy. Unfortunately, many congregations view community ministries as serving "others" and do not have people directly affected by problems involved in the initial design.

The organizing committee must truly seek to discern the possible community-wide issues that the congregation can work on in developing its advocacy ministry. Identifying issues that affect the life of the community must take place in the context of working directly with the local community. Identifying issues that are near to the heart of the community cannot be done in a vacuum or just by reading the latest *Newsweek* magazine! This step becomes a block for some congregations in developing their advocacy ministry. Thus, the next guideline becomes critical.

2. Design an extensive listening and discernment process to ensure that community problems are truly heard and understood. To discern the problems that affect the larger community, members of the organizing committee need to go outside their church walls! They need to do their homework by going door to door, interfacing directly with members of the community. Ideally, each congregational member involved in this data-gathering process should talk to at least fifty people in the community. The purpose of the visits is for the congregational members to meet their neighbors, get to know them by name, and listen to their dreams and concerns for their families and their community.

The framework for listening visits is simple. After introducing himself or herself and explaining the purpose of the visit, the visitor needs to ask the person he or she is visiting the following baseline questions:

* What are your hopes? for your family? for your community?
* What concerns do you have? for your family? for your community?
* What community issues/problems would you be willing to give your time and energy to work on?

Other questions can be developed by the committee, but remember that the purpose of the visit is not to get responses to a long laundry list survey. The visit is the means by which the congregation begins to develop a relationship and potential partnership with its neighbors and community.

Some congregational members are not comfortable in calling on their own members, let alone strangers! Therefore, someone who has visitation skills should provide some role-playing exercises and training to help the members who will be doing the neighborhood visits to learn such skills as how to begin and end the visit, how to listen, and how to ask questions. In brief, the persons making the visits should have the opportunity to rehearse a visit so that they can feel more assured. Another way to enable members to gain a greater level of comfort and confidence in their visitation is to have teams of two people make the call, such as teaming a person who is experienced in calling with someone who has never made a neighborhood visit.

A clear time frame should be developed for the group's visitation schedule. After every member of the calling team completes visits, then the group should gather to reflect on and to discuss their visits. This is a time to affirm people's experiences in their visits, especially if it was a new experience for them. It is a time to share what helped people feel more comfortable or uncomfortable in their visits so that they can learn and grow from their experience. Finally, it is a time for the group to share what they heard from the people they visited. From this last topic, the group will most likely end up with a laundry list of hopes, dreams, problems, and issues.

The next step is for the visitation members to go back to the people they visited to provide feedback to them about the information that was collected from all of the visits. This is an opportunity to let the people in the community know that "they have been heard by their visitor-friend," and for the church folks to build upon the relationship that was initiated in the first visit. At this time, an invitation should also be extended to the person to participate in small group discussions on the information collected. These small group meetings can be set up in people's homes, in local community settings such as a community center, or perhaps in the church building. The purpose of these meetings is to continue to build community between the church members and the neighbors they visited, to get additional feedback and support for the information that has been collected, and to begin the process of identifying, clarifying, and prioritizing the significant problems impacting the community that the church and community could possibly work on together.

After this extensive listening process, several primary problems and concerns will emerge. At this point, congregations may still be tempted to set up social service programs. But they are less likely to limit programs to services since they have a personal understanding of the suffering of neighbors and their commitment to seek changes.

Unfortunately, few congregations have any practical experience in selecting advocacy issues and developing effective strategies. For congregations without experience an outside facilitator from a denominational office, a local seminary, or a training organization like the Midwest Academy (Chicago) can be brought in to lead the congregation and community members through this process. A facilitator who is skilled in community building, power analysis, issue selection, and strategy development is an invaluable tool in helping a group not only to think and ask the right questions, but also to gain the insights and skills to develop an effective advocacy ministry.

3. Build in opportunities to help congregations reflect on their ministries. Since the largest number of congregations that got involved in advocacy did so after they were more in touch with community problems through getting to know people, it is important to build in opportunities to reflect on ministries and directions. Perhaps every six months to a year, staff, leaders, and volunteers should be asked to reflect on directions of the program and what else could be done.

With a strong rootedness in the community, the congregation can work in partnership with its neighbors to define and analyze the issues that impact the community and develop a short- and long-term strategy to cause system change on the issues it is determined to effectively address. The analysis and strategy development look at several questions: What are the risks? Who are our foes and potential partners? How will this strategy build up our resource base and power? What systems are we trying to change? How will this process empower the community? How will this improve the community in the long term?

4. Challenge Christians to understand and use their power. Since American Christians usually do not talk about our power, we do not use it as often and as well as we could and we should. Thinking and talking about power and how to use it with love helps Christians increase our impact in society. The best way to have these discussions is in the context of prayer and biblical reflection.

Congregations that want to develop an advocacy ministry must begin with the fundamental belief that advocacy ministry is essential and integral to the life and mission of the church. Advocacy ministry cannot be considered a "fringe ministry" that belongs to the congregation's social ministry/outreach committee. This is the kiss of death for most congregational-based advocacy ministries!

Rather, using power with love must be preached from the pulpit, studied in Bible study, and discussed at church council meetings. Leadership must be sought from the senior pastor (most congregations have only a pastor!), Bible study teachers, and members of the governing body. The members of the organizing committee need to begin this process by educating their fellow congregational members and the key leaders about the role of advocacy ministry in the life of the church (e.g., Bible studies, sermons, adult forums, retreats). Without the public support of the key pastoral and congregational leaders, any effort to develop an advocacy ministry will not be sustained in the long run.

5. Develop a long-term vision on a spiritual foundation. An effective advocacy ministry requires stick-to-itiveness leadership. We will not change unjust systems overnight. The struggle to bring about divine justice and righteousness is not only about developing a short-term or long term process strategy or program, or a management of ministry issue. Undertaking an authentic advocacy ministry is a faith commitment. Advocacy ministry is part of our life and vocation. Development of an effective advocacy ministry requires vision and commitment to the building up of the Kingdom. Advocacy ministry is a lifetime walk with God!

There is no simple shortcut formula for developing an effective congregational-based advocacy ministry. It requires the congregation to be bold in its vision, committed to its mission, willing to give significant time, energy, and resources, to be a risk taker, and to work in partnership with its larger community. Most of all it requires faith in the knowledge that God's righteousness and justice will prevail. Our most practical advice is spiritual—to live the belief that justice is central to our calling as Christ's witness in the world.

PART 3

Resources

CHAPTER 7

Raising Money for Church and Community Ministries

Cathy A. Potter

"I'll do anything but ask for money" is a frequently expressed sentiment among volunteers, and, of course, it reflects the attitude commonly found in Church and Community Ministry Projects. However, we need only think about our own households or business budgets to recall the role that money plays in accomplishing important goals. All we need is "enough" money; whether our expectations are small or great, success will—in virtually every case—depend on acquiring adequate funding. We must learn to think of fund-raising as a solution, not a problem.

Consultants working with the Church and Community Ministries tried to communicate the fundamentals of start-up in community-based fund-raising, and encourage and empower volunteers toward fund-raising action. Why were some projects able to acquire the resources they needed to accomplish their mission while others had little success? Although many circumstances might explain why fund-raising did not happen, in this chapter we focus on successful efforts and possible explanations.

From my perspective, success begins with two foundations. The greater the perceived community need addressed by the project and the greater the individual and collective volunteer commitment to meeting that need, the more successful fund-raising efforts will be. Success is measured here not by numbers of dollars but by whether "enough" resources were raised to implement the planned project.

We have seen in Church and Community Ministries that volunteering "begets" volunteering; this giving of self creates more of the same. This could also be said of asking for money for the cause and receiving money. This happy experience produces a rush of excitement, confidence, and willingness to ask again. Success is a powerful motivator.

This chapter presents some basic guidelines for successful church and community social ministry fund-raising, along with some illustrations of how individual Church and Community Projects raised funds.

Fund-Raising Defined

The classic definition of fund-raising describes a process beginning with visibility, which creates awareness, then interest, support, commitment, and eventually contributions of time or money or both. Visibility—public relations—is a critical first step in the fund-raising process and, in itself, plays a valuable role in the success of your project.

Public Relations—The First Step Is Telling Your Story

"If a tree falls in the forest and no one is there to hear it, does it make a sound?" That old question can be translated with relevance to emphasize the importance of an effective public relations program for community ministries. These ministries are doing great work—God's work—but if no one knows about them, do they exist? Yes, they exist for the sponsors and the clients. But it is likely that if a ministry is not known beyond its clients, it will not be able to exist for long—certainly not for the long haul. Where would volunteers come from to replace those who move or who burn out? Where will money come from to keep the project going? In fact, where will new clients come from?

Leadership and a Plan

When we think about public relations, we often put media first. Newspaper, television, and radio coverage are an important element of PR, but not the most important or the first element to consider. Your public relations efforts shape your ministry's identity, and the board must take responsibility for this. A project needs a public relations chairperson who is a board member. Enthusiasm, commitment, and willingness to work are the main criteria in choosing a chairperson. Usually, people who want to do this job can learn the rest.

Working with the planning committee, the chairperson should first prepare an "on paper" plan, complete with a timetable. The plan should consider communication for all of the ministry's potential constituencies but place internal communication (with clients, volunteers, and partners) as a priority. If this is handled well, word of mouth—the most desirable of all public relations tools—will be launched.

Other elements of a PR plan include agreement on who "you" are and what "you" do, the establishment of your identity. A logo, or symbol, is a valuable tool to develop, and it should be used on project stationery, newsletters, brochures, and so on. If possible, a newsletter for volunteers and supporters, and perhaps clients, is suggested. It is proof that your project is really happening and, at the same time, lets you get your message out to those involved. It can also be used outside your organization in the community.

Speakers Bureau

Another recommended early PR activity is a Speakers Bureau. This is an effective yet inexpensive way to tell your story. Think of all the clubs and organizations in your community that need monthly or even weekly speakers. A mailing telling a little about your project and offering to provide a free program is sure to bring positive responses. Follow-up phone calls to each organization to arrange for presentation dates are well worth the time invested.

The talk should be short and allow time for interaction with the group. Visuals and handout material multiply the impact. Try for creativity in presentations. Speakers for the Education for Conflict Resolution project in North Manchester, Indiana, take two trained volunteers along who role play a conflict situation and its successful resolution. Face-to-face personal contacts made at these presentations lay the groundwork for future fund-raising efforts and can help recruit volunteers.

Memberships

A public relations committee should also consider the idea of memberships in your ministry and potential membership-building campaigns. You want to try to spread the ownership of your project to all potential allies, volunteers, and other supporters. Membership can be an excellent vehicle for this. Membership and fund-raising drives can be effectively operated together, especially when a project or organization is well established in a community.

The Literacy Coalition of Kokomo-Howard County began an annual direct mail membership effort five years ago. Board members and other volunteers provided membership lists of many clubs and organizations, and the group saturated the community with a letter offering the opportunity to be a part of the Coalition. At the beginning, multiple membership levels were offered, from $5 to $500 or higher. Today, the minimum level is $10, and the average membership contribution is $20. They started with 60 members (15 of whom were on the board); today, they have about 3,000. Their goal is to have 8,000 members, and they are always looking for different lists of names to add to their mailings. (Their newsletter also includes a membership reply form each month.) Board members get together to personalize annual membership solicitation letters by thanking those who have been past supporters with handwritten notes. They believe this has helped upgrade memberships to higher levels over the years.

Special Events

Special events can be important elements in a public relations plan. Many times they are conceived as fund-raising activities. However, the effort usually needed to accomplish such events suggests that they should have a dual purpose of publicizing the project as well as raising money. In fact, the visibility benefit is most often the prime reason for special events.

The annual Spelling Bee held by the Literacy Coalition in Kokomo is an excellent example of a special event that raises money, and is extremely valuable in the visibility and awareness it provides. It is a community event with wide participation and receives excellent media attention. Corporations, clubs, churches, and other groups enter teams for a $40 fee, a good time is had by all, and the mission of the Coalition is in the spotlight. The Spelling Bee raised about $2,500 last year.

Media Relations

Positive relationships with the media in your community are invaluable aids to your ministry projects, and there is little or no cost for this publicity. Key in establishing good media relationships is remembering that news coverage must be on their terms. Sometimes volunteer community organizations feel the paper or the TV station "ought to" or "should" use a story on their event. That is not the case because only the media decide what to cover or publish.

Your job is to provide all the information on the media's terms, in a timely fashion, and make using it easy. For example, if you have an event you want covered that includes a meal, invite media representatives as your guests. Always provide every assistance for reporters in getting their story. Also, the story is theirs, and they will cover as much or as little of it as they wish. The ideal arrangement is to establish a personal relationship with a reporter who seems to have special interest in your project. Always contact that person and, if possible, deliver information to that person directly. Never address a news release to a paper or station without a specific name attached—it is very likely to be lost. Also, find out the daily deadlines for the media in your area, and do not phone or visit them around those times.

As you work with media contacts, you learn quickly what they expect from you. Also, in some communities, organizations like Women in Communications offer handbooks or special workshops on how to work effectively with the media. These can be very valuable.

Public relations/communication defines your project for others and spreads its impact. It is a vital first step in fund-raising.

Fund-Raising—Getting Started

Early experiences with Church and Community volunteers indicated that most of them used the term *grant writing* instead of *fund-raising* when they talked about acquiring resources to perpetuate their ministries. This, unfortunately, represents a fairly common understanding of fund-raising—you prepare grant proposals and write letters asking for money and you will succeed, a perception that rarely fits reality. Quite fortunately, the basic concepts of community-based fund-raising are such

common sense that volunteer boards quickly see their logic. There is
nothing like common sense to turn on volunteers.

Total Board Responsibility

Volunteer boards first need to accept fund-raising as a total board responsibility. You are the "experts" on your project; you are the most
committed to your project. Quite honestly, if fund-raising is not successful, you must deal with the implications of the lack of success. A fund-
raising chairperson should be recruited from current board members, or
an obvious choice from other interested volunteers can be brought onto
the board. This person will want and need a subcommittee of enthusiastic helpers, but the relationship with the board (and the public relations
committee) should be strong.

Case Statement

Develop a case for support; this is your vision. The fund-raising and
public relations committees can take the lead here, but the board is the
think tank and must approve the final statement. Basically, you need to
decide the following:

- Who are you and what is your mission?
- Why is it important?
- Who will benefit from the accomplishment of your mission?
- What do you need and plan to do?
- How much will it cost?
- What will be the result of your efforts?

    This information needs to be written on paper, even in a simple and
brief form. You need to know the answers to these questions before you
can productively think about who might want to support you. This task
helps to focus your board and at the same time provides an outline for
any fund-raising publications or letters you may want to create. It could
be said that preparing your case statement will "set you free." The focus
this provides helps you to see the possibilities of your ministry, and
potential funding sources, more clearly.

Constituency

Next, you must develop a list of prospects who are potential donors. Here is where logic comes in as you think about your constituency. Who is most likely to care about your vision and want to support it? Is it that big foundation in another city or state? Or might it instead be someone closer to home who understands the needs you are trying to address and who sees the potential benefit of your project in personal terms?

Consider that in 1992, 81.9 percent of all charitable giving in the United States came from individuals, 4.8 percent from corporations, 6.7 percent from foundations, and 6.6 percent from bequests. *Grant writing* and *fund-raising* are not interchangeable terms. In fact, grant writing is only one avenue to financial support and neither the easiest nor the most successful road to take. Your best prospects are individuals, undoubtedly in your community, who care. Who are they, and do they know your story? They need to learn about what you are working to accomplish, and they should be offered the opportunity to share in your mission by providing resources. A broad-based, representative board is a real asset as you work to develop your constituency.

A Fund-Raising Plan

Develop a plan with a time line for your fund-raising efforts. It does not need to be fancy; just include what you are going to do, when you will do it, who is responsible, and a completion date for each task. Set realistic goals for each fund-raising effort. You already know why you are raising money; be sure you know how much is needed to fund your vision.

Ideally, your project's public relations committee is active, effective, and coordinating with your fund-raising efforts. In fact, a brochure that establishes your project's identity can also serve as a fund-raising piece. If you are clear about who you are and what you are doing, and you have established credibility in your community, you are ready to begin an individual gift campaign.

At this point the fund-raising committee should go back to the total board for help in creating a list of prospects. A brainstorming session on who might logically care about your cause is productive, builds board members' ownership of funding, and can actually be fun. Do it early when enthusiasm is high, and remember the principle of no bad ideas in a brainstorming session.

Asking Individuals for Contributions

The fund-raising committee needs to refine and detail the list of potential prospects created by the board and plan visits to these individuals to ask for their advice and support. (This type of effort is often referred to as an annual fund campaign, or a capital campaign when a one-time gift for a building or endowment fund is sought.) Supporting materials need to be prepared, such as the case statement brochure, and a response card and return envelope.

Each board member, each fund-raising committee member, and any other logical volunteer should be assigned three to five prospects to visit. This spreads the task and the joy of fund-raising. Always solicit people most likely to be interested prospects first. They can have the opportunity to share in your project, and early fund-raising success is tremendously encouraging as you continue your campaign. Keep to your timetable. Do not let your personal contact effort drag on too long.

Active Care Develops Community (ACDC) in Deer Creek, Indiana, used this model to raise about $18,000 for their community center project. Deer Creek is a town with no schools or businesses, and the two partner churches are the only focal point for a feeling of community. As the name indicates, their project was to develop a sense of caring community, and they created many programs toward that end. They decided they wanted to build a community center and reserved almost all their CCP grant funding for that purpose. Of course, they needed additional money and undertook a unique person-to-person campaign.

They started with preparation of a case statement that presented the usual information, including what had already been accomplished and a timetable for the building plans. Pictures were included, and it was especially designed for the process of solicitation. The five-member board of directors then recruited twenty selected area residents who they felt cared about the project and would be willing to ask for money. This group was trained and divided into teams of two, and each team made visits. Their goal was to talk with every individual or family who lived within a five-mile radius of Deer Creek.

Basically, they accomplished their goal. They offered special incentives for various levels of gifts, which they feel was a positive factor in the campaign. The largest gift was $5,000, and there was at least one $1,000 gift. A plus in this effort was that the process itself contributed to ACDC's goal to build a sense of community. It was important that everyone in the area have the opportunity to contribute, and appropriate that a broad-based group of people be recruited to do the asking.

Another ministry, the Education for Conflict Resolution project in North Manchester, Indiana, organized a personal "ask" campaign. They were raising money for operations and used only board members as solicitors. A local retired professional fund-raiser helped them with their planning and provided a training session. Each board member was to visit three to five individuals, although most were disinclined to do this.

In the end they feel the effort was only modestly successful (they raised $6,600). Perhaps a factor was that they had developed some other excellent sources of funding, so urgency of need was not present. A plus was the positive experience of one board member who forced himself to make a call on a local merchant, even though he was reluctant to do so. To his surprise and delight, he received a pledge of $100 per month support—a commitment that resulted in $600 for the program.

Direct mail is another way to ask for financial support. This type of fund-raising works best when you have access to large lists of prospects, through your own membership or perhaps through board connections. Keep in mind that direct mail can be quite expensive due to printing and postage costs, and that a 3 to 5 percent response rate is considered to be exceptionally good. Your letter should be carefully crafted, and personalized if possible. The Literacy Coalition membership/annual appeal effort discussed earlier is an excellent example of effective direct mail fund-raising.

Special Events

Special events are a revered traditional form of fund-raising for churches (i.e., the spaghetti dinner and the bazaar). Many times these events do not raise large amounts of money when the amount of work involved is considered, but they are comfortable and they have great community-building and social benefits beyond the dollars realized. Special events for fund-raising are most valuable when public relations/visibility for the cause is also accomplished. An example might be a health fair and blood drive combined with a bazaar or supper if your project is a community health clinic. The Literacy Coalition Spelling Bee discussed earlier is an outstanding Church and Community Project example.

Consider the possibility of recruiting other organizations to sponsor fund-raising special events for your project. Who might be willing to do this? How about some of the clubs and organizations for whom you have provided speakers? Most of these groups have philanthropic causes, why not your project? Mediation Services of Tippecanoe County, Indiana, hopes to get this kind of help from fraternities and sororities or other Purdue groups next fall. Your partner churches and organizations are obvious prospective helpers. ACDC does not have its community center quite ready to go, but it already has commitments from church partners to hold a fund-raising community breakfast at the center on the third Saturday of every month.

There are as many possibilities for fund-raisers as there are people to think of them. Do not shy away from them, especially when they also promote your cause or if the work is being done by another organization. Just keep in mind that they are not likely to raise large amounts of money.

Gifts of Materials or Services

Most community projects think of soliciting gifts of materials and services. It is "doing what comes naturally." However, this idea deserves mention here precisely because it has been used so much by Church and Community Projects. Projects involving construction have had gifts of materials and of time from electricians, plumbers, carpenters, and many do-it-yourselfers. Other gifts include trees, a handsome sign for the ACDC community building, and the services of an artist who contributed her time and ability to create two large recognition plaques for Lacon Area Community Center. The Lafayette Transitional Housing Center had the printing of its annual report contributed—not through a printer, as one might expect, but through the public relations department of the employer of one of its board members.

The message here is, keep thinking and keep asking. Remember to acknowledge these gifts of materials and services in the same way that gifts of cash are acknowledged. It is easy to overlook them when lists of donors are prepared.

Product Sales

The classic product sale to fund a cause is Girl Scout cookies. Representatives of the Girl Scouts will tell you that the sales process itself is part of the learning program of the organization, and anyone who has been through it probably agrees. This same principle should be considered when deciding whether to try raising money for your community ministry project through product sales. The best product sales are ones that also advance aspects of the program beyond fund-raising.

The Lafayette Transitional Housing Center has sold an attractive, awareness-building lapel pin over the past two years with great success. Each year the center grossed $15,000 and netted about $8,000 (at $10 per pin). The jewelry quality pins were marketed through area boutiques, the area council on the aging, many local churches, and a booth at a large regional shopping mall. Each pin came on a card telling that pins were being sold nationwide to support projects that addressed the homeless problem. Another visibility-enhancing product sale was the sweatshirts, T-shirts, and hats created by the Lacon Area Community Center for the "walk" for the center fund-raising event.

A unique product sale was sponsored by the Burnettsville Community Youth Center. Working with a dealer in a nearby town, they held a monthly recycling collection morning at the center. Materials brought in were sorted by volunteers into receptacles provided by the dealer, who then purchased the collected goods. It was a win-win fund-raiser because of the environmental benefit and the educational factor.

Fee for Services

Many times we do not think of client fees for programs created by a nonprofit organization as fund-raising. A number of Church and Community Projects have found fees, based on ability to pay, an important factor in their current financial health and their potential future stability.

Mediation Services of Tippecanoe County and Education for Conflict Resolution (ECR) both charge fees for training groups of people in conflict management and mediation skills. These services might be provided to corporations, clubs and organizations, groups of attorneys, and so on. In essence, the services are needed and important to people who are able and quite willing to pay. This helps make possible the provision of free mediation services and training for individuals or groups with little or no financial resources. Whether paid or not, the mission of these conflict resolution programs is being addressed by these training sessions.

ECR provides an additional service, for compensation, to its community. When a former school building was converted to a Town Life Center, the director of ECR was asked to manage the center, and ECR offices were provided in the center. The director also works part-time for the Community Foundation, which has its offices in the center. This sharing of facilities and personnel is a wonderful partnering in the community, and adds a great measure of stability for all involved.

Lafayette Transitional Housing Center logically charges a fee for service, since part of what it provides is housing. The center is required, by the terms of HUD funding, to assess fees on the basis of an ability-to-pay formula. A commonly held attitude in this country is that people in need both want to be and should be active partners in improving their situation. Many also feel that giving someone something for nothing may not necessarily be a favor. A sliding scale fee for services might well be a plus as you ask for contributions because your project will be viewed as one that helps people help themselves.

Grant Proposals

If you have lots of time, write grant proposals, but read grant guidelines very carefully and consult with corporation or foundation representatives, if possible, to ascertain whether your project fits their funding requirements. An outstanding how-to reference for grant writing is the article "Write on the Money: The Basics of Effective Proposal Writing, from Content to Structure to Length" (*Currents*, October 1988, pp. 10-17).

Funding cycles are important with corporations and foundations, so even though your project might be fundable, the money could be as much as a year away. Decisions usually are made by groups whose decisions are then subject to further approvals. Also, corporations and foundations are subject to economic cycles, which may mean promised funding could be delayed or canceled.

Corporations and foundations closest to home are the ones most likely to have interest in your program. This principle applies to all fund-raising—the best prospects for giving are those closest to the cause. With individual prospects this might mean board members, volunteers, or even clients.

Corporations

Your best chance to raise money from corporations is through personal contact and with a specialized approach. Mediation Services of Tippecanoe County has had significant success through the efforts of one committed board member. This person prepared a proposal, which had as its base a classic case statement. He sent a two-page overview letter to selected local corporations, then called for an appointment and presented the longer document. He generated more than a dozen significant contributions (several at $1,000) from some of the largest and most prestigious corporations in the community. This means more than just the money; it means this program is accepted by the power structure, a definite plus for the future. At least one firm made a second $1,000 gift.

Church Partner and Denominational Support

There has been some concern that church partners would consider Church and Community Projects a financial threat as a potential drain on their budgets. In reality there has been great variety in the response of partner congregations once the original CCP grant funding ended. Support ranges from none to contributions from groups within partner churches to dedicated line items for CCPs in church budgets. Some church partners have promised regular fund-raising events—often community dinners or breakfasts like the ones planned in Deer Creek. The Education for Conflict Resolution project has had two of its partner churches tithe to it from gifts they received through bequests.

Church and Community Projects should be encouraged by the results of a national study done for Independent Sector based on 1991 figures and reported in the May 18, 1993, *Chronicle of Philanthropy*. It shows that "America's religious congregations are increasing their charitable work, even as the amount of donations they receive is declining." Churches are not only involved in providing human, health, and other public and social services themselves; they are helping to fund outside projects that address these same needs.

Denominational support has been strong for CCPs, ranging from a $1,000 Presbyterian grant for playground equipment at the Deer Creek Community Center to many levels and forms of support for operations from across the spectrum of denominational committees and foundations. In general, applying to denominational entities for programmatic or specific project funding makes sense. This fits the "close to home" phenomenon. Your application will undoubtedly be reviewed by people who understand what you are trying to accomplish and empathize with the people you want to serve. Social ministry projects should explore denominational funding early in the fund-raising process.

Planned Giving

It seems inappropriate to think of planned giving (bequests and trusts) for Church and Community Projects as long as they are young and tentative. Prospects are unlikely to want to give to a cause, no matter how committed to it they are, if they cannot be sure the program will exist in the long-term future.

Education for Conflict Resolution is working to establish an endowment fund through the Community Foundation in North Manchester. With this organization as the repository and manager of gifts, donors can be assured that their wishes will be followed. Contingencies can be established so in case ECR no longer exists at the time the estate matures, the foundation will allocate the gift to another cause of the donor's choice. Special benefits for ECR in a relationship with the Community Foundation would include broad new visibility through inclusion in the foundation's publications and access to matching funds currently being provided to community foundations by Lilly Endowment.

Economists agree that the single largest intergenerational transfer of wealth will occur in this country in the next twenty to thirty years. Most predictions of the amount involved range from $5 to $10 trillion. Individuals who care about the causes being addressed by Church and Community Projects will be among those who transfer this wealth. Projects need to explore appropriate ways to make bequest opportunities available to them. Community foundation possibilities should be explored.

Thanks and Recognition

Once a donor is acquired, no matter what the size of the gift, a special partnership is created. Timely acknowledgment, appropriate recognition, and nurturing are essential to the fund-raising process. As our mothers taught us, we must thank and appreciate those who give us gifts or treat us well.

Thank-you letters can be prepared by anyone delegated to this task, and should be signed by the most appropriate person. Many times, this is the chairperson of the volunteer board that runs the project. Another thank-you letter or note (perhaps handwritten) can be sent from the person or persons who asked for the gift. Recognition for giving might mean inclusion on an "Honor Roll of Donors" published in your newsletter, invitations to special activities, or small mementos for donors (T-shirts with logo of project, pins, etc.). In some cases, the name of the donor is placed on the piece of equipment provided or perhaps the room furnished.

The Lacon Area Community Center is a classic and creative example of recognizing donors. Everyone knows of buildings named for very generous donors. The Lacon group expanded on that idea. They offered parts of the building for naming—windows, doors, and so on. In this small community, the ownership represented by this idea was wonderful and successful. Another recognition vehicle used at Lacon was two tree-shaped plaques at the entrance of the building. Leaves on one bear the names of regular donors to the project, and leaves on the other name those memorialized by others through contributions to the community center.

Stewardship and Cultivation

Stewardship is the responsibility assumed by those who accept gifts to use them wisely and in the manner promised. This responsibility includes being able to account for expenditure of dollars received to the donor and to the public in general. It also involves such matters as timely accomplishment of projects and proper maintenance of facilities or equipment provided by gift funds.

Cultivation includes thanks and acknowledgment, but more than that it involves treating donors as part of the project family, keeping them up to date on progress and, to the extent they want, letting them be involved. This step in the fund-raising process often leads back to the beginning, to the giving of another gift.

Conclusions

Church and Community Projects are overcoming the reluctance to ask for money. Volunteer commitment to the cause and the urgency of the need being addressed seem to be important determining factors in fund-raising success. Many great ideas have been birthed and nurtured by Church and Community Projects, and fortunately, volunteers have not been willing to let these ideas go.

In review, the best prospects are individuals, and the most cost-effective and successful form of fund-raising is the person-to-person "ask." In a 1985 national study commissioned by the Rockefeller Brothers Fund, "The Charitable Behavior of Americans," a major reason people said they gave was *that they were asked.* Conversely, when asked why they had not given, 14 percent said no one asked, and 23 percent said they did not get around to it.

People give from their discretionary resources, not their grocery money. If you ask and receive a gift, your cause and the donor benefit. If you ask and the answer is no, your situation is no different from what it was before you asked. For the sake of your cause, please ask!

CHAPTER 8

Denominational Leaders: Blind Spots and New Openings

Carl R. Smith and Philip C. Brown

In our experience with the Church and Community Project, we found hope for many churches in recognizing the misperceptions of and about denominational leaders. We recommend an ecclesiastical vision checkup. Blind spots among the principal actors in the congregational-denominational dialogue contributed significant problems in our work, and yet we found that the misperceptions also offered new and creative possibilities.

At the heart of our problems we found serious stereotypes. The clergy, both denominational leaders and pastors, significantly underestimated the willingness of laity to engage in outreach ministry programs. At the same time we found many laity are waiting for leadership, looking for the go-ahead signals from their pastors or judicatory staff. When the signals do not come, the responsibility is not with the laity but with the timidity of the clergy. Much of our data suggest that the clergy's stereotype of the reluctant laity inhibits developing community ministries.

In a similar way, the church members' stereotype of denominational leaders as program-pushing bureaucrats equally inhibits creativity. Denominational leaders see their world quite differently. These leaders bring high ideals based on a desire to be faithful disciples. They feel the lash of ugly stereotypes that diminish their energies, dissipate their talents, and deny their spiritual resources for the church.

Our views reflect the experiences of thirty middle judicatory staff who serve closest to the local church, in the dioceses, conferences, associations, presbyteries, and other metropolitan or area-wide organizations of a dozen denominations in Indiana and Illinois. During the Church and Community Project, these denominational leaders shared their experiences, responded to questionnaires, and shared their faith journeys.

The data from them corroborate our experiences: We feel stretched between several different religious structures only marginally connected and all too often in tension with each other. Despite this stress, our experience in the project suggests ways to develop mutual, positive working relations among local denominational representatives, pastors, and local church leaders.

Shredded Denominational Connections

From our data and our experience we recognize that denominational identity is not a primary concern for most church members. Skipping across denominational lines is a common exercise. The Presbyterian Church is a case in point:

> A recent survey of the Presbyterian Church (USA) found that fewer than half (43 percent) of its members and only 61 percent of the pastors had been Presbyterian all their lives....The theological identity of the Presbyterian Church has become blurred, as the "boundaries" between Presbyterianism and other major denominations have become less distinct during the past decades. (McCarthy 1992)

Although denominational ties with congregations are now fragile bonds, this condition reflects a relatively recent shift in American society. We recall the heady days of national unity in and after World War II when mainline churches were growing, and denominational labels were important for congregational and personal identity. In that period success for many Americans was confirmed by "climbing up the denominational ladder" from Pentecostal to Baptist to Methodist to Presbyterian and finally to the Episcopal Church (Pope 1942).

Today, denominational switching does not follow the old pattern. Denominations are arranged not in a pyramid but as a scattered melange without widely accepted authority.

Wade Clark Roof's description of the baby boomer generation reflects the broad shift in values that has negative consequences for denominational loyalties:

> Boomers have not just known pluralism, they deeply value it.

Tolerance and respect for others are widely affirmed as basic values, to be honored in religious as well as other contexts. For them, the American practice of speaking of religion as a "preference" assumed a taken-for-granted quality. What else could it be but a personal choice? No generation in America's history was ever more exposed to or more devoted to pluralism as a social and religious quality. (Roof 1993)

Though mainline denominations no longer dominate the religious landscape, they have not vanished, as some reports would suggest. Nationally and locally, they are still important players. They supply funds to start new parishes, certify clergy, supplement low salaries, and manage health and pension funds for thousands of employees. As religious bodies with their publications, educational institutions, and many layers of meetings, denominations are keepers of the religious heritage and cultural continuity for loyal members. Spiritually and emotionally, they offer a broad and continuing sense of family amid an increasingly mobile and alienated society.

In efforts like the Church and Community Project, we see the problems and the possibilities of denominational staff in middle judicatories. They are accessible to congregations and provide a personal/professional link between the local church and the larger organization. Middle judicatory leaders are contemporary circuit riders—knitting each local church into resources and concerns that transcend its own sanctuary walls.

Denominational Leaders in the Crossfire

We can see the crossfire of misperceptions by looking at the ways that denominational leaders see themselves and the ways that others perceive them.

Middle judicatory staff feel as if they are indeed caught in the middle of the crossfire between warring expectations. We have clustered these as tensions in three areas: between institutional push for program and personal commitments to service; between serving immediate needs and urging essential change; and between the frustration of working with resistant laity and the excitement of new ministries with creative lay leaders.

Middle judicatory staff report feeling that their denominational employers expect them to sell the programs of the national church and, indeed, measure their professional success by the acceptance of these programs in local churches. Congregations, on the other hand, look upon judicatory staff as a resource to help solve local, often internal problems. Said one middle judicatory staff member, "Our time is overcommitted to promote denominational programs, but we are frequently interrupted with congregational crises. Then we must decide which has priority." In this tension, denominational expectations take top priority, but congregational troubles cannot be ignored. In the squeeze, attention to community ministries was pushed into the margins of their energy and time.

Although in their job descriptions, the program pusher image had validity. Yet in the Church and Community Project we discovered that outreach ministry was their personal priority, but usually absent or low status in their job descriptions. Even though social action ministries were not given priority by the denominational system, the staff voluntarily participated in the program. We asked why they did it.

The answer lay more in the spiritual pilgrimages they followed than in the jobs they hold. Most of these leaders share a passion for social ministries because of their faith. Further, we discovered that these faith commitments came not in their formal education but in lessons they learned in the formative years of life.

Twenty-four denominational leaders in the Church and Community Project wrote spiritual autobiographies that revealed times when the seeds of their social concerns were planted. Asked when they first became aware of human need or social injustice, twelve reported their first awareness occurred at home as a child, three recalled the civil rights movement, two remembered youth work, and the others recalled isolated personal experiences.

Significantly, the seed of passion for social justice was sowed outside their memories of church experiences. Long before their professional church responsibilities, most denominational leaders recalled personally transforming experiences, most at home from lessons learned as a child at the mother's knee.

Further, these denominational leaders felt that they sometimes paid a price for their beliefs. Those who chose to participate in the Church and Community Project observed that their "interest in social justice relegated them to a minority position in the denominational hierarchy and among the church membership generally." They perceived themselves as participating for reasons that they thought might be contrary to their professional interests, but they acted because of strong commitments embedded in their most basic values.

Living with a Split Personality

Middle judicatory staff also report pressures of differing agendas in their visits to local congregations. When the staff come to work with a congregation to help solve internal problems, they are seen in positive terms. They report the words used by others to describe their contributions:

listener	cheerleader
counselor	facilitator
organizer	consultant
cultivator	teacher
resource person	pastor
motivator	energizer
preacher	processor
enabler	newsprinter

As long as the conversation stayed focused on the congregation's problems and stated in the congregation's terms, relations between the congregation and judicial staff were upbeat. But the judicatory representatives reported a distinct shift in attitude when they put on a denominational hat and attempted to challenge the congregation to see the world in different ways and to change the status quo. When they asked congregations to adopt new, denominational programs, staff felt they were described with negative and sometimes abusive language, such as:

bureaucrat	manipulator
intruder	lawgiver
"one of them"	insensitive
authority	"liberal"
messiah	"pinko"

Denominational representatives reported these contradictory role labels wherever they went. One staff member spoke for many others when he reported that whenever he visited a parish, for whatever reason, some members assumed he was there to push new program. "It always takes some informal, personal talking time to get the barriers down to where the conversation can begin," he said.

This discovery reflects a painful irony, that denominational leaders' passion for social justice alienated them from the primary denominational agenda, on the one hand, and from congregational needs, on the other. The internal demands of both the denomination and the congregations were legitimate, but he Gospel also commends the denominational leaders' faith-based urge to extend ministry to the world outside these institutions.

Facts Are Gone, Feelings Remain

The negative language might be more understandable if the denominational leaders felt that their own mistakes had earned it. But for some church members the appearance of a judicatory representative triggered old resentments. Most judicatory staff recalled conversations like the words of a church member who justified the church board's resistance to a new program by referring to "what the denomination did to us back in '43." The denominational leader protested, "But I hadn't been born in 1943." His defense did not register, he recalled.

The long memories of church members often include old battles with the cherished if inaccurate dates, personalities, and causes long lost in the mists of history. Only the anger remains. As ethnic rivalries have shown us, the pain of these old wounds can survive the changing of leaders and even the passing of generations. When the denominational leader inherits these bitter memories, no pleas of personal innocence will set the feelings aside.

Thus denominational leaders working with the Church and Community Project felt in the crossfire from all directions. From denominations they felt pressure for being evaluated by their effectiveness in helping local churches accept judicatory programs. From local churches they felt pressure to deal with existing parish problems, not denominational priorities, and blamed for ancient conflicts and unresolved feelings.

In the midst of these conflicting expectations, denominational leaders reported mixed messages about their commitments to social concerns. All sides gave permission for social involvement, *provided it did not conflict with other priorities that already took full time.* Little wonder that denominational representatives felt like jugglers keeping denominational, congregational, and social concerns in the air at the same time.

Staff Misperceptions

It is hard to engage in self-reflection when you are running flat out, which is the way most judicatory staff describe their lifestyle. Perhaps this frame of mind contributes to their pervasive clichés about the laity. Consistently, we found among both denominational leaders and local pastors that *clergy underestimate the interest of church members in social ministries.* But a wide variety of data from the Church and Community Project show that church members are more willing to engage in neighborhood outreach than the clergy expect.

In our attitude surveys we found that denominational staff and local clergy significantly and consistently underestimated church member interest in community ministries. For instance, on questions of giving a high priority to church programs to help the needy in the community, 73 percent of all laity said that such programs should be a high priority for the church. However, denominational leaders expected that only 43 percent of the laity would put a high ranking on aid to the needy. Religious professionals set themselves up as different from the laity. Indeed, clergy did rank responding to human need more highly than lay members (90 percent), making their anticipated distance from the laity all the more pronounced.

In expectations of support for social reform, the discrepancy between clergy expectation and membership response is even sharper. About half of the laity (51 percent) thought social change was an important mandate for the church. However, clergy expected support from only 21 percent of the laity. By contrast, we found that clergy accurately assessed lay interest in the importance of other church programs, such as nurturing spiritual life and fostering education, especially for children.

In short we find a pessimistic stereotype that pervades the culture of religious professionals about the commitments of laity toward social ministries. This stereotype is clearly unsupported not only by the responses of laity in questionnaires, but also by their commitments to develop and sustain strong ministries in the Church and Community Project.

Yet in the dissonance of misperception lies the seeds of a self-fulfilling prophecy. When pastors were initially contacted to invite their congregations to join the Church and Community Project, they pointed to the reluctance of their laity as the most frequent reason why the congregation could not participate. One-third of invited clergy responded, "I would love to get involved, but my laity are opposed." We do not have information in those churches where the religious professionals refused to enter the project. But in every case where we have these data, rank-and-file members are more willing to participate than the clergy are willing to ask.

The data show that laity are far more willing to support community ministries than their leaders expect. As one cleric confessed, "It's time we admitted that we were wrong, and get on with the outreach ministries together."

Separated by the Same Language

Further, we learned from the Church and Community Project how misperception leads to failure in communication. One dramatic example is the definition of *justice*, a key word in discussing and developing social ministries.

Theologically, throughout the project we lifted for dialogue our faith in a "God of justice." From the questionnaire we found that clergy and church members had very different concepts in mind. The majority of the laity (60 percent) defined justice as a personal virtue, "That I should be just and fair in all my dealings." Clergy overwhelmingly believed that the "God of justice" expected the whole church to be involved in seeking justice, which "should support groups that are working to end inequality and oppression" (95 percent). We struggled with a wide perceptual gap. For the clergy, God's justice implies systemic change; for the laity, God's justice is a personal responsibility.

Some clergy trace these differences to seminary education. Some put the cause at experiential frustration when they discovered that the sources of injustice were unchanged by giving food at Thanksgiving, toys at Christmas, or clothes to the homeless shelter. We noted how often these differences emerged in parish life in sermons, counseling, committee discussions, and board meetings. Yet even in these face-to-face meetings, we discovered that key words continued to mean different things to speaker and listener.

Throughout our work, we were struck by the need to develop common language based on shared experience. We found these apparent differences diminished when participants had a common base of shared experience where they learned to respect and trust each other—beyond talking, we worked together. Then when we talked, sometimes we found that participants really agreed, and some conversations led to more articulate disagreement. But from working and talking together we found an appreciation of each other even when we could not agree. In these experiences our stereotypes were destroyed, or simply forgotten, buried under much stronger common bonds.

The Minority Voice of Pluralism

In the Church and Community Project, denominational staff discovered the networks of smaller groups make up every congregation. Judicatory staff came to feel that these "minorities," not dominant leaders or simple majority rule, offered hope for new insights and creative programming. In developing social ministries, for example, when these subgroups were encouraged to speak, they provided bridges between those who understood justice as an important goal for the church and those who saw justice as primarily an individual responsibility.

Denominational leaders learned to look for these networks and protect the variety of viewpoints across and within subgroups advocating social ministries. Nobody had the sure answer. Everyone needed help from others with different viewpoints and commitments. In the language of social critic Robert Hughes, we should be glad for a rainbow of values, or what he calls multi-culturalism. Multi-culturalism, in this approach, expects us to look and think across the boundaries of race, language, gender, and age, without prejudice or illusion. It directs our attention to boundaries and borders, both for their own fascination, and even more as the hope of the future.

From the experience of working with several congregations, middle judicatory staff increased their skills in defining the boundaries of agreement and the specific foci of dissent. They learned to ask and answer, "What does the other person really believe?" and "Where is compromise possible?" Until churches recognize the stands of the various parties in church decision making, they are reduced to guessing, which, as the data gathered by the Church and Community Project show, is an untrustworthy guide.

Beyond Stereotypes Passing in the Night

Throughout the research developed by the Church and Community Project, we found evidence of dissonance between the views held by laity and religious professionals (as seen by others; see Williams 1991). "Common wisdom" proved inaccurate and sometimes destructive, either by laity or by clergy. These mindsets blocked initial communication and, over time, could become self-fulfilling (and self-defeating) prophecies.

To break this cycle, we developed simple guidelines. Although judicatory staff generated them, they could be useful for laity and pastors as well.

1. *If someone says that laity are not interested in social ministries, do not believe it.* Church members are more willing to become engaged in social outreach than either pastors or denominational leaders previously believed.

2. Conversely, *if someone suggests that judicatory staff are interested only in pushing programs, do not believe that, either.* Church professionals at all levels are as committed as laity to developing their spiritual lives and nurturing the spiritual lives of others.

3. *When you have a chance to explore your differences, take it.* Protect it, promote it, and use it as a basis for creative new possibilities. With trust and mutual respect, address the barriers of language when the opportunity arises. Although our experience shows great gaps in the language of faith used by clergy and church members, we are also living proof that shared experiences can transcend our differences and energize our work.

4. *When you can affirm the views of others, do it.* In the face of

tension and misunderstanding, the importance of affirmation cannot be overstated. In a phrase that became a mantra among us, "There is more to your work than leading cheers, but try it whenever you can."

5. *If you want to build a new future, begin by sharing your relevant past.* In addition to conceptual knowledge, everyone brings memories of earlier relationships, perceptions, and faith commitments. Let this history come out. Encourage it. Signposts for the future are planted in the past.

In short, drop stereotypes, explore differences, and weave your separate experiences together. Perhaps the last was most important. Whenever we took the time to stop pressing forward long enough to listen to the spiritual autobiographies of others, new dimensions of commitment developed among us. In listening we lost our stereotypes and discovered a strangely human-divine mix of trust, respect, and affection.

These disciplines of listening are difficult and risky forms of faith in action. When we used them, clergy and laity felt embraced together in the love of God. Then sharing in community ministry seemed a natural, almost inevitable, consequence.

CHAPTER 9

Partnership for Community Ministry

Reflections

Sally A. Johnson

Partnership has been a key to expanding the resources and impact of
social ministries in the Church and Community Project. Fortunately, we
have some excellent models of churches reaching into their communities
to embrace a common cause in the spirit, if not the words, of Jesus.

In Springfield, Illinois, a Presbyterian church of 160 members with
about 80 attending worship in a small multipurpose sanctuary identified
three groups they wanted to reach in their community: frail elderly
people, families, and young children in potentially abusive situations.

In Indianapolis, two large congregations of well-educated, upper-
middle-class white members wanted to reach out to their neighbors in a
low-income African-American neighborhood just a few blocks away.
Yet they were well aware that they could not know on their own how
best to help.

Across town from them, three small Methodist churches in a yoked
parish looked around at the neighborhood they had shared for many
years and found the housing stock deteriorating rapidly. They decided to
begin rehabilitating homes for and with low-income residents, with the
ambitious goal of community renewal through physical improvement.

Each of these churches felt a call to minister in the community, and
each faced the challenge of responding with limited resources to seemingly limitless need. Each found an answer in partnerships. Throughout

the Church and Community Project, congregations have expanded their resources by reaching out to their neighbors through building partnerships—not only with other churches, but also with local businesses, social agencies, governmental groups, and an array of other interested institutions.

Forms of Partnerships

In one sense, every partnership is unique, formed by the intentions and commitments of two or more groups and their respective leaders. But at the same time, we can describe several general types of partnership, based on our experience with midwestern church-based social ministry programs over the past four years.

An *institutional partner* is the most closely involved in the ministry project, formally affiliated through representation on the governing board of the program. The partner shares full responsibility for the project with the originating church: decision making, funding, and program design and oversight. Often institutional partners have been with the program from the beginning. In many cases, two or more churches first form a partnership and then develop their ministry together.

In Lafayette, Indiana, for example, St. Thomas Aquinas and St. Boniface Catholic churches decided to create a joint community ministry. Together they considered various issues and chose to develop transitional housing for homeless families. When members of Shalom United Church of Christ read in the newspaper about the new ministry, Shalom joined as a third partner. All three partners were represented on the board of directors, and they fully shared responsibility for the success of the program.

A *program partner* contributes resources of some sort to the ministry on a continuing basis, without full responsibility and board membership. Most program partners become involved either during the planning process or after the ministry has begun. The village board of Bradford, Illinois, provides space for the Bradford Church and Community Project in the village hall at no cost. World Relief supplied a teacher for a year for English as a Second Language classes offered by the Marshall Square-Douglas Park Family Education Center in Chicago. The Garfield Park Church of Christ Men's Roofing Group donated their labor on several occasions to the housing rehab efforts of the Fountain Square Church and Community Project in Indianapolis. In each of those cases, the organization did not share institutional responsibility for the project, but contributed to the program on an ongoing basis.

Finally, an *advisory partner* plays a role similar to the program partner, but for a limited time. Advisory partners step in to provide expertise or other resources at a particular time in the project's development, but they have no continuing commitment to it. Bradley University assigned students to carry out community research for Community Action Ministries in Washburn, Illinois. The Historic Landmarks Foundation of Indiana advised Active Care Develops Community, in the town of Deer Creek, on how to seek state protection for an old park area at the edge of town. Like program partners, these organizations lent their expertise to the community ministry program—but on a short-term basis.

Styles of Partnering

In our experience inner-city churches often have a kind of entrepreneurial spirit about their community ministries. They tend to form loose and temporary coalitions with groups that can offer them particular resources for the project at hand rather than long-term partnering relationships. In Chicago, the Sweet Holy Spirit Baptist Church created a C.A.R.E. Center, which they operated in a storefront building adjacent to their church. At various times they called on schools, a grocery, an eye clinic, a community college, and other churches to help them in their outreach.

By comparison, *small town congregations* more often turn to other churches and settle in to work together for the long term. In Deer Creek, Indiana, the Deer Creek Presbyterian and Faith Lutheran churches—the only two churches in the community—formed a partnership for community ministry before they ever decided what to do. They have sponsored a variety of community-building events and recently built a community center, and they continue to plan for future activities—together.

The Hope Presbyterian Church in Springfield (see the case study following) created a *cooperative ministry center.* Through the pastor's contact they found three service agencies that addressed their three areas of concern: St. John's Hospital Adult Day Care provided care and socialization for elderly Alzheimer's patients; Interfaith Counseling was an independent, ecumenical agency serving families in the community; and the Parent Place worked to prevent child abuse through various programs, including a parental stress hot line and a drop-in day care program that offers respite to parents of young children.

Hope and its partners then sat down together and designed a new building—a church and community center combined. Each agency has its own space, built to its own needs, and the church has a large new sanctuary and additional facilities. The four partners share the decisions and expenses of operating the building.

Sources of Partnerships

The most obvious for finding partners is *proximity*. In Canton, Illinois, the Catholic church and the United Church of Christ were across the street from each other, though most members had never been inside each other's building. They joined together to create a program for helping senior citizens with health insurance and Medicare. In Indianapolis, the First-Meridian Heights Presbyterian and Northwood Christian churches were half a block apart; it was natural for them to form a partnership. In Burnettsville, Indiana, the First Baptist Church drew the other two churches in town (Brethren and Christian) into planning for an after-school program.

Some churches find partners within their *denomination*. The Cornell Baptist Church in Chicago received help from two other Southern Baptist churches in another state. Also in Chicago, the Immanuel Lutheran and Lutheran Chinese Christian churches turned to Lutheran Child and Family Services to help staff their outreach to Indochinese immigrants. *Neighborhood clergy groups* are another source of partners. In Lacon, Illinois, four churches came together through their pastors' network: one United Church of Christ, one Methodist, one Catholic, and one Lutheran. Through this cooperation, the pastors found their own group strengthened by the experience of working together.

Sometimes there is a *history* of cooperation that can provide a base for new partnering. In Bradford, Illinois, the Leet Memorial United Methodist Church and St. John the Baptist Catholic Church had opened their facilities to each other at times of crisis over the years. When Leet wanted to develop a program employing teens to do home maintenance for senior citizens, St. John's was a natural partner. Some programs need particular kinds of *expertise*, and agencies can provide it. When the Community United Church of Christ in Morton, Illinois, created Day-break, Inc., to provide day care and respite services for frail elderly people, they sought advice and referrals from We Care, Inc., a local agency providing meals-on-wheels to seniors.

Finally, some groups connect with partners through *individuals*. The board of the Literacy Coalition of Kokomo-Howard County (Indiana), initiated by St. Luke's United Methodist Church, includes individuals who are active in local businesses, labor unions, and organizations. Although the members are not official institutional representatives, they provide access to their respective groups. The director of HANDS, a ministry with deaf and hearing impaired people begun by Ridge Lutheran Church in Chicago, has been widely active in the deaf community and brings a variety of connections to this new organization.

Risks

As with individual human relationships, partnerships for ministry take time and work to build and bring some risks for the initiating church. Chief among these is the risk of a *diminished sense of ownership* on the part of the congregation. As long as church members bear the full responsibility for a ministry, they may be more conscious of it and more deeply involved. When they are the only source of money, volunteers, and other resources, the program demands more of their attention: It sinks or swims based on their efforts.

Even as partnership expands the resources available for the program, it can dilute the church's sense of ownership. It is easy for the church's involvement to dwindle to keeping a member or two on the board and perhaps taking an occasional special offering—especially if the church shares with several institutional partners in running the program. At the same time, partnership makes the program itself stronger and more viable.

St. Luke's United Methodist Church of Kokomo created the Literacy Coalition as a ministry of the church. Given the needs of the community and the quick success of their program, the organization grew rapidly. Now nearly four years old, the Literacy Coalition is an independent not-for-profit agency with a broad and effective program and United Way funding. St. Luke's still has a representative on the board, and individual members volunteer; but beyond that the program has become owned by the community rather than the church.

Sustaining commitment on the part of the church requires planning and effort even as the program itself does. Church leaders who want to maintain their church's investment need to keep the program visible within the congregation. Bulletin boards, newsletter articles, Minutes for Mission during worship, inclusion in pastoral prayers, reports to the church board or council—measures like these will help. Leaders should actively recruit volunteers for the program and should recognize and celebrate their work publicly in the congregation.

The initiating congregation will also have to recognize that sharing ownership with partners, especially institutional partners, will sometimes mean negotiating the vision. When partners genuinely share in the responsibility for the program, they also share in the creativity. If there are foundational principles that the church does not want to give up or modify, they should be codified in a constitution that includes a statement of purpose. Beyond that, the church should be open to building a shared vision and program.

Divided loyalty can be another risk. Representatives to the project's board who are central to their own organizations may not give this project top priority in their own time and efforts. When Washington Street Presbyterian Church in Indianapolis formed Partners for Westside Housing Renewal, they sought to create a network among related agencies in their neighborhood.

The agencies responded by appointing their directors to represent them on PWHR's board. But because those persons were staff and therefore already heavily invested in their individual organizations, for many PWHR was their second (or lower) priority. After a time the board reorganized itself to include more laypeople and representatives of the community at large—and the board's energy increased. As much as possible, partner representatives should be people who are free enough from other staff or volunteer responsibilities that they can make this program their top priority.

Building partner relationships can be difficult, especially when the groups are dissimilar. Four congregations located within a block of each other came together to choose a project for their neighborhood. Three appeared quite similar in outward characteristics: Their members were white, educated, middle-class people drawn from the same community. The fourth was an African-American congregation. All four had difficulty in building a viable partnership; in the words of one person, it was "like trying to dance with four left feet." Looking more deeply, we found that despite the similar appearance of three of the congregations, each of the four had a different kind of history and self-image.[1] Alike on the surface, they were very different underneath. They persisted, and—through building relationships, sharing clear goals, and creating a strong organizational structure—they now sponsor a successful ministry to seniors.

Relational difficulties can be particularly tricky when the partner groups represent *different cultures*. The First-Meridian Heights and Northwood churches (the second opening example) needed to build partnerships with neighboring black churches in order to gain insight and access for ministry in that community. Douglas Park Covenant Church, in Chicago, and its sister church, La Iglesia del Pacto Evangelico, worked hard for three years to forge a partnership that would sustain a ministry with Hispanics in the neighborhood—and enhance the relationship between the congregations as well. The outward program was the Marshall Square-Douglas Park Family Education Center, but an inward goal was the partnership itself.

At HANDS in Chicago, mentioned earlier, the board is composed of deaf and hearing members who have found that the cultural gulf is as wide between them as between any ethnic or color groups. It takes time and persistence, a sustained respect for the other group, a willingness to risk, some fights, patience, and good humor to build a cross-cultural relationship.

Benefits of Partnership

Finally, however, partnership between churches and other community groups can bring benefits that far outweigh the risks. Most obvious is the *expansion of resources* available for the ministry. Partners can bring financial support, volunteers, facilities, in-kind goods, expertise, and clients, among other advantages. The three small Methodist churches mentioned in the third opening example are now carrying on a $250,000 housing rehab program, using up to a thousand volunteer hours per month. They have made partners with everyone from churches to realtors to the county corrections department (which provides probationers as volunteers). For them, partners have made ministry possible on a scale they could have only dreamed about alone.

Partnership often brings *ecumenical awareness and relationships*. Church and Community Project leaders and volunteers say ecumenical experience is one of the strongest benefits they have found in their community work.[2] The UCC and Catholic churches in Canton, the Presbyterian and Lutheran in rural Indiana, the Methodist and Catholic (and Lutheran and Baptist) in central Illinois—all have found deep satisfactions in working together. These newfound relationships often last into the future and spawn new kinds of shared ministry.

And partnership can bring greater *community visibility and credibility* for the program—and for the sponsoring congregation as well. The Manchester Church of the Brethren in North Manchester, Indiana, had felt ostracized for decades because of their historic peace stance. When they set out to apply their commitment to peace and reconciliation to their hometown context through a program of conflict resolution in the grade schools, they found a variety of churches and community groups willing to join with them. Before their formal program ever began, their partnering process demonstrated new credibility in the community and brought reconciliation to the church and its neighbors.

The more visible and connected the church's outreach programs become, the more the community takes them seriously. When four churches in Washburn, Illinois, teamed up and took a close look at their community, they began asking such questions as whether the subsidized housing in town was administered properly. Soon the town board approached them to ask their help in opposing a nuclear waste dump that the state proposed to locate at the edge of town. In another town, one agency director expressed surprise and delight at a church's invitation to partner in a community ministry, saying, "We never knew the church cared as we do."

Partnership can provide crucial resources and invaluable experience for a congregation that seeks to reach out in social ministry. Partnership does more than answer an immediate circumstance—it builds community. For churches that care as much as their neighbors do, that is exactly where they belong.

1. We used an analytical framework of five self-images by which congregations describe their history of community involvement: pillar, pilgrim, survivor, prophet, and servant churches. See "Congregational Self-Images for Social Ministry" by Carl S. Dudley and Sally A. Johnson, in *Carriers of Faith: Lessons from Congregational Studies*, edited by Carl S. Dudley, Jackson W. Carroll, and James P. Wind (Louisville: Westminster/John Knox Press, 1991), pp. 104-21.

2. Taken from a survey conducted by the Center for Church and Community Ministries in the fall of 1990. Reported in a presentation to the annual meeting of the Society for Scientific Study of Religion and Religious Research Association, November 1991, entitled "The Impact on Volunteers of Participation in Social Ministry Projects," by David P. Caddell and Sally A. Johnson.

Case Study

John R. Buzza

Introduction

As a pastor working with the Church and Community Project, I was
fascinated by and especially involved in partnering with others in community ministry. To expand my own experience I talked with the leaders
of ten other church-based ministries in the project. I asked each, "What
kind of partners do you have, and what's the history of your working
together? What has stayed the same and what has changed in the experience? What have you discovered in partnering, and what advice do you
have for others?"

As a partner in a ministry, let me note one complication: In our
state, the words partners and partnership are technical legal terms, which
involve legal liabilities between organizations. When I use these words,
I do not include the legal meaning but the kinds of working relationships
that Sally Johnson has already described (above). In our church relationship with three social service agencies in our building we developed a
legally binding "Joint Operating Agreement," which included the lines:
"Nothing in this agreement shall be deemed or construed to create the
relationship of principal and agent, partnership, or employer and em-
ployee between the parties hereto. Each agency or party is an independent contractor with regard to its own operations conducted in or on the
premises." Although the church may be casual with language, working
partners must be careful in the documents prepared.

First Learning: Partnerships Required Work

All of us agreed that strong partnerships do not happen by accident.
They take intentional effort to develop trust, share a vision, plan together,
and sustain the relationship over time.

Good partnerships are built on trust. In our case, partners were the
natural outgrowth of previous relationships. When we invited three
social service agencies to join in the renovation and expansion of our

church building into a community ministry center, we were building on past ties. The pastor had served on the board of directors for two of the agencies, including one, the day care program, which was already meeting in the church. The third agency was well known because one of the church members was making extensive use of its services. For all four partners, personal contact engendered trust that provided the foundation for working together.

In other communities the foundations were laid by sharing the community vacation church school, cooperating on community projects, or simply having a long history of living in the same community. One project leader noted that partners are "out there, if we only took time to notice, but we all have a full plate of things to do."

We worked for a clear vision of ministry. Sometimes the clarity of vision precipitated partnership. In two ministries for senior citizens that I contacted, churches crossed significant differences for a common cause. In one case they joined to help seniors fill out written forms for medical care, insurance, taxes, and the like—a vision that brought together a United Church of Christ, a Roman Catholic church, and a local hospital. In the other town, leaders who were concerned for elderly people joined together from half a dozen churches, and as they worked together, they expanded to respond to the needs of all ages in a wide variety of programs.

Detailed planning helped partners work together, according to eight of the eleven ministries. Unquestionably, the planning itself was helpful. But I also recall that since it was required by the Church and Community Project guidelines, the planning process provided a common format and sometimes a common enemy—like a denomination—that we could agree to oppose.

The *sustaining nurture of mutual support was essential.* First came the original enthusiasm of a shared vision and desire to accomplish something meaningful—the energy in the start-up phase of the ministry. Later, as the ministry developed and we faced the realities of daily operations, intentional maintenance of the relationships became more important.

An unbalanced partnership can be unhealthy. One project leader recalled, "When the chips are down, in emergency situations, you have to go where the resources are." In her case the resources resided primarily in one of the four partner churches, and she explained, "It's been difficult to maintain a true partnership when there is a decided difference in the strength and resources among the congregations. It is difficult for the church that has greater resources not to become paternalistic, like a parent-child or big brother relationship."

A different ministry, when faced with the same gap in resources, developed a creative solution: One of the churches provides more funding, while the other church provides the facility. Even this arrangement, however, requires a continual dialogue between the partners to keep the sense of partnership balanced.

Partnership requires even more effort across racial boundaries. In one interracial mix of churches, a leader recalled that "the only church that would have had the resources to do it would have been one of the white churches, but since we are serving predominantly black youth, I don't think that would have worked." They survived when they redefined resources as "whatever is essential to this ministry," including location, personnel, contacts, space, finances, and volunteers.

Second Learning: Partnership Paid Off

Financial advantages were the most obvious for us and for all the ministries with whom I talked. Financial partners began with the Church and Community Project and included denominations, foundations, individuals, and others that provided an expanded financial network. In addition to the sources of money growing, the believability of the ministry with those funding sources increased as partnerships expanded. Some established funders even insisted upon broad representation as a criterion for support and, generally, getting contributions from individuals and businesses was easier when more partners were involved in the ministry.

Having more people is another obvious and delightful advantage of expanded partners. Particularly in the initial stages, more people mean more energy, more volunteers, and more ideas at a time when brainstorming problems is necessary. In my survey of ministries, the ratio is consistent: the more people involved, the greater their chances of success.

Mouth-to-mouth advertising is another advantage of partners. From the small towns to the congested urban settings, word of mouth remains important in generating both support for the ministry and clients to be served. The more narrowly defined the target population to be served becomes, the more helpful it is to have broader representation on the board.

Credibility of the ministry is increased by expanding the board, especially when it also includes participants from the target population. For example, HANDS, a ministry with deaf and hearing impaired people, expanded its board of directors to include a deaf person, and then elected a deaf president and hired a deaf person as executive director. At that point they could reach more directly into the deaf community and became a more trusted "voice" for deaf people in the larger community.

Public challenge is easier to handle with community support and wide participation. When support for the ministry is broad based, with community leaders actively involved, legitimate complaints can be dealt with openly and creatively. Complaints that are unfounded or generated by a small segment or a single, unhappy person can be seen in context and dealt with appropriately. One ministry reported that its board was actually strengthened as it responded to a disruptive single individual who was trying to undermine the ministry. The community support that rallied behind the ministry provided the context in which to confront the situation creatively.

Internal conflict within the ministry can also be more easily addressed if the board is broadly based. When staff members need guidance or severance, or when individual board members mishandle situations, broad-based boards have a better chance of avoiding judgments based on personality and power. I heard how difficult it is, for example, for a board made up of members of only one church to fire an inefficient director, especially if the director is also a member of that church. It may be hard to share the problems "in public," but board members remembered pulling together under stress.

Credibility, in short, is a powerful experience that helps to generate the self-sustaining energy for ministry. As partners provide good feedback from the community, the ministry builds credibility, and those working in the ministry are encouraged to continue. As pastors we like to think that faith is the strongest motivation that supports the ministry, but I discovered that good community feedback certainly helps as well.

Third Learning: Partnerships Come at a Price

Time is the greatest cost of partnership, in my experience and in my interviews. When I asked what advice about partners they would give to others, nearly everyone said, "Be honest about the time involved—it's more than we expected, especially in the beginning." Once the ministries got organized and the board responsibility shifted from operations to policy development and general oversight, the time demands decreased. But building trust and finding the common vision took time.

The *loss of control* is a second cost. When a ministry develops partners, the partners will inevitably influence all aspects of the ministry. We felt this at two levels. At the decision-making level, actions are slower, corporate decisions more complex, and participants must intentionally represent a constituency greater than themselves.

At another level, loss of control takes a more subtle form. Sometimes fundamental beliefs are at stake in seemingly simple decisions, and once these surface they remain a part of the dynamic tension of doing business together. For example, in our ministry among the four partners were a Presbyterian church and a Roman Catholic hospital. The hospital sponsored an adult day care center, which would use the church fellowship hall. In the planning process, one of the Presbyterians asked if the Catholics would expect a crucifix on the wall of the day care center, "the way they are at the hospital, you know?"

The matter was acknowledged but not resolved, and it never came up in the board again. However, in time a crucifix "appeared" in the Presbyterian church hall, but because of the good feelings among partners, it is seen by all as a positive symbol of personal trust and larger faith that makes the partnership work. Not all matters are so easily solved. In some cases, church participants denied their old symbols to accomplish their new goals. The sacrifice of old symbols and comfortable patterns is often the cost of building strong partnerships.

Fourth Learning: Partners Challenge the "Church"

Everyone I talked with had stories of changes that were precipitated by partner relationships. In our case we experienced a gradual shift from a church and religious orientation to a civic and community alignment of ministry. We saw this shift in the changes in board membership from church members to more community members. Seven of the other ministries reported a similar increase in the number of community board members. Perhaps symbolic of the shift, one ministry celebrated when it became a United Way Agency, fully claimed (and funded) by the community. Then staffers wondered if the ministry had lost something precious.

One sequence was reported from a successful ministry in which half a dozen churches constructed a new community center. One leader recalled the issues this way: "As additional community needs became obvious, we struggled to recruit broader representation in our board and our programs. In my time on the board we debated whether to serve alcohol at a fund-raiser, and then whether to remove the 'churchy-type' banners from the walls when someone found them offensive, and someone else worried about funding. Then we wondered whether to reserve a place for a pastor on the board. Until this year we thought, 'Well, yeah, we do.' Well, then we determined that it didn't have to. We started with the clergy, and now it's all lay, and we're doing just fine."

On the one hand, I want to stand up and cheer. In these partnership ministries, laity have taken over from clergy, and community people should share the leadership with church members. Theologically, I agree that the church should be witnessing to the love of God by our ministries in the world. Personally, I agree that we enact our faith by touching the lives of others—the gift of giving as we have received.

On the other hand, I worry that something precious may be diluted and possibly lost when there is no clear expression of the faith foundations for these ministries. When all the disciplines, banners, crosses, and clergy are excluded, or popularized until they have no religious meaning, how will the newcomer know the source of this energy? And who will be the next generation of "giving as we have received"?

In these partner ministries I see a parable of the struggles of mainline churches across the country. In putting our faith into action, we have shaped national voluntarism and public philanthropy. In our efforts to be inclusive of others—as partners in the Church and Community Project, for example—we may have neglected or obscured our own uniquely Christian roots. I hear the echo of those who say that "our actions should speak louder than our words," but do they?

I am energized by the experience of partnering, the living of our faith in ministry with others. Without it, the church is irrelevant and our growth in faith is stunted. At the same time, as Jesus was both a healer and a teacher, healing alone is insufficient in this spiritually hungry world. We can share with partners in the act of healing ministries of compassion and justice, but we must also maintain the uniquely religious affirmation of our spiritual foundations.

PART 4

Why, What, and How of Church and Community Ministries

CHAPTER 10

Why Churches Choose Particular Ministries

Carl S. Dudley

Background

The Church and Community Project began working in the spring of 1987 with forty congregations that roughly reflected a profile of denominational Christian congregations (size, location, membership composition, etc.) in the four geographic areas of Indianapolis, northern Indiana, central Illinois, and Chicago. These churches engaged in a planning year (1987-88) to help them, with community partners, to develop ministries in one of six "survival areas" of education, health, housing, hunger, unemployment, and world peace. With continuing support from the Lilly Endowment we provided consultants, workshops, and seed funding for three years (1988-91) for thirty-two ministries that received support. In the first published report of this project, *Basic Steps toward Community Ministry* (The Alban Institute, 1991), we carried the list of initial congregations and the ministries they planned at that time.

Twenty-five of these ministries took root and matured over the period of consulting and seed funding, and only one was discontinued in the first year without financial support. Four years later we have discovered that one of the discontinued ministries (with elderly people) returned— when the board dissolved for lack of funding, the participants reorganized and continued their own ministry, thus maintaining twenty-five continuing programs. In the years since we began working with leaders of these ministries, virtually all of the projects have developed a second and third generation of leaders, raised funds, changed primary staff, and watched the majority of pastors relocate. They all succeeded in reaching their primary ministry goals, surviving, even thriving, through a combination of anticipated and unexpected challenges.

Although in *Basic Steps* we listed the ministries alphabetically, in this chapter we reflect upon our discoveries about selecting and supporting various ministries in the areas of education, elderly, housing, community improvement, and advocacy for systemic change. In each section we suggest the core faith commitments and organizational connections that other churches might find useful. For those who want more detailed information, in the appendix we offer a thumbnail sketch of the status of the twenty-five ministries continuing in the fall of 1995 (plus one that closed after 1991), including a brief description, a feel for the ministry, and a few comparative statistics about volunteers, staff, budget, and participation.

Three Preliminary Influences in Program Decisions

Before we look at findings from each program area, we note three broad factors that influenced all selections: first, the influence of seed funding; second, the continuity of program; and third, the emphasis on helping people rather than solving problems.

Seed funding—up to $20,000 annually for three years—had the anticipated effect: It empowered church leaders to imagine new community ministries. Less money might have constricted the choices for some churches, but we have no examples of possible ministries that they left unexamined for lack of financial support. To that extent we can learn how churches might decide if they were relatively unfettered by financial constraints.

However, the infusion of funding had an unanticipated downside as well. Some congregations felt the burden that the options were too many and the expectations too great. Congregations were properly afraid of launching programs that they could not sustain. The seed funding was large enough to encourage dreaming, but insufficient to sustain continuing professional staff.

In fact, these ministries have succeeded financially far beyond any expectations—projects based on $600,000 annual investment now sustain budgets close to $6 million annually. But these totals are disproportionately inflated by several large projects, and the vast number of continuing ministries are modest and sustainably sized (see details in appendix).

More typically, Church and Community Project staff worked with a dozen congregations in the same area in 1992 and following—without any seed funding. With this group we had a higher percentage of churches that succeeded in launching ministries; only their hopes and their failures were more modest, and their budgets were sustainable from the beginning. *Although seed funding had a unique impact in the Church and Community Project, you can find ample resources in every congregation to develop its own community ministries.*

Second, despite the fear of some church leaders and the hopes of others, participating congregations did not undergo radical change. Rather, churches chose ministries that were consistent with some aspect of congregational history and leadership experience. In developing social ministries, you can intentionally emphasize particular elements from a wide variety of faith convictions and social commitments carried by members in their congregational consciousness. *To energize ministry, you can build new programs by using selective continuity of satisfying elements from past congregational experience.*

Third, in considering program options, church members were consistently more concerned with helping people in their neighborhoods than in solving problems in their society. *To generate advocacy for broad issues, help members focus their concerns for real people they know or with whom they can empathize.*

I. Education: First Choice for Churches

Given the range of community concerns that suddenly became possible ministries with available seed funding, we were surprised to see educational concerns dominate church choices. Nine of the twenty-five congregations chose education as their primary focus for ministry, and virtually all the others included educational dimensions.

Apparently for most churches, educational programs provide the easiest and surest bridge to mobilize church energies into social ministries. Through observations, interviews, and reports from participants in these ministries, we note the rationale and motivation for educational ministries that others might find helpful.

1. Theologically, educational ministries express congregational commitments as teachers of faith and moral values and as resources to develop the maximum human potential in each individual. You can

mobilize virtually any church to generate educational programs to both teach faith and develop character.

2. Experiential, educational ministries reflect church commitment to the intimacy of family bonds and the link between faith and culture. Virtually all minority and immigrant churches in our program emphasized educational programs. You can mobilize congregational energies in educational programs for children, youth, parents, and the next generation.

3. Practically, educational ministries are imaginable since all churches have experience in teaching the faith. Churches have facilities for educational purposes, know how to get educational volunteers, and can keep budgets within reach. More than just teaching, educational ministries provide an outlet for the gifts of a wide variety of church and community volunteers.

In short, educational ministries are the easiest to mobilize since they combine Christian commitments and practical action from members who want to give to people who need help. In an educational program you can generate commitment to make an impact in the present and an investment in the future. Although these programs are diverse and often tenuous, many develop into strong, effective, and substantial ministries. Beyond the programs with a primary emphasis on education, some aspects of education appear in virtually every church-based social ministry.

From our experience, *you will find educational programs the most appealing as a first step for congregational development of community ministries.* As you seek broad-based support for social ministries, consider beginning with an educational design—the most universal and natural foundation to mobilize typical congregations in response to community problems and needs.

II. Elderly Ministries

Elderly programs were the ministries developed by four of the twenty-five congregations, including the one that closed after 1991 and the one that reopened by the tenacity of participants. These programs included care centers, hot meals and other services, respite care for home givers, and advocacy about conditions affecting elderly people. In addition to primary programs, another half dozen churches included the elderly within a larger focus. Together they shared theological perspectives and personal hopes for the ministries they developed.

1. Theologically, churches are highly motivated to honor "our parents" (which includes all elderly people), respect the family, and care for those most vulnerable. You can mobilize energy for elderly programs with an appeal to Christian compassion in the church and in the community.

2. Experiential, elderly ministries respond to an immediate, visible need. Especially as the median age of churches increases, golden-agers dominate the changing demographic profiles of denominational churches and the communities they serve. You can generate support for an elderly program from elderly people themselves, and even more from middle-aged caregivers who are often current church leaders.

3. Like education, elderly programs are relatively easy to imagine. As a kind of fellowship program, churches have ample experience and available space and equipment. Although elderly programs may at first appear simple and manageable, they are more difficult when they include securing licenses, raising money, supervising staff, and dealing with similar unexpected detours and booby traps.

Project Daybreak, sponsored by a community church (UCC) in Morton, Illinois, had grand ambitions, but scaled back to provide simple home respite to caregivers with elderly people in their families. A program that first seemed too simple, then impossible, now has been absorbed naturally into the lifestyle of several community congregations.

From all the different options for ministry, *you will find that ministry with the elderly has the most universal appeal. You can launch a ministry with the elderly in all social locations, ethnic cultures, congregational sizes, and denominational backgrounds.* The combination of Christian compassion and aging persons was widespread and well matched throughout the two-state area.

III. Housing Ministries

Housing programs require specialized and demanding activities and, therefore, rarely appeared as a minor theme in other programs. You do it all the way, or you do something else. Although our four continuing housing ministries show a wide variety of styles and supporting structures, we found the theological commitments and personal motivation remarkably similar.

1. Theologically, housing ministries require not only a concern for individuals but also an investment in neighborhood welfare. For these ministries you need support for particular families and for physically improving the community as expressions of faith in action.

2. In practice, housing ministries are more demanding than other ministries. They require large capital expenditures, continuing organization, and a variety of professional people. You will need very different kinds of organizations, skills, and resources for rehabilitating occupied homes, rebuilding empty homes, maintaining an overnight shelter, and developing long-term transitional housing.

3. Compared to other church-based ministries, housing ministries require more human, physical, and financial resources from supporting congregations—at least in the initial phases. Since these programs are so structurally and theologically demanding, you often find more passion surrounds a housing ministry from church members divided in their support, some for and others against.

4. In addition to the programs they support directly, housing ministries are often involved in community-wide advocacy for social concerns in both public and private housing. For example, Partners for Westside Housing Renewal called itself PWHR (pronounced "power") to reflect its commitment to a strong advocacy network for low-income home owners.

Housing ministries are not for everyone, but *you can mobilize a housing program where the need is clear, the resources are available, and the commitment is solid and sustainable.* Housing ministries produce the largest financial turnover and support the greatest number of staff, both professional and volunteer (see the appendix). They have a profound impact on the neighborhood with ripples throughout the church and community. For example, with support from both Catholic and Protestant churches, the Lafayette Transitional Housing Center goes far beyond shelter to include job training for youth, family life education for young parents, and counseling for troubled families. With cost and risk, the impact increases.

IV. Comprehensive Community Ministries

All five comprehensive community improvement projects were located
in areas with definable boundaries. When other churches had similar
goals, they used more issue-focused approaches, such as housing rehabilitation or local school improvement. But some churches chose a comprehensive, community-wide ministry; we saw a variety of settings from
the most agrarian town of Bradford to C.A.R.E. in the pressures of inner-
city Chicago.

   1. In their beliefs, a community or parish theology motivated comprehensive improvement ministries. In this faith the church, or partnership of churches, accepted responsibility to enhance the quality of community life. You can energize such ministries when church leaders help
to find and allocate resources that improve the community for all residents, unifying people in common cause across their differences of class,
culture, race, and religion.

   2. In practice, these comprehensive improvement ministries did
more than solve problems: They provided common space where aggregate individuals and groups remembered they were community. When
you can help your neighbors feel ownership of common space, the variety of programs they bring separately becomes a symbol of something
larger in which they are all included.

   3. Leadership in comprehensive community ministry is provided
more by generalists although specialists are sometimes needed, more by
amateurs although professionals are essential, too. Since these programs
bring together such an array of community problems and resources, they
especially need people who represent their diversity and yet are committed to their unity.

   Comprehensive community programs do not spring up everywhere.
They happened not from design, but from necessity, supported by a
parish-wide theology. They do not need massive resources or clear
social issues. *As leader in a definable but diverse area, with multiple
needs, modest resources, and a faith that embraces the community, you
can launch a comprehensive improvement ministry.*

V. Justice Ministries

Advocating systemic change was the chosen focus for four church-based ministries. As reported in other chapters, we asked all programs to advocate for systemic changes when they found unjust or oppressive conditions. These four ministries that took advocacy as their primary focus were initiated by distinct minorities within their congregations, and yet they were able to receive official and often enthusiastic support from their churches. We note here the rationale that made such support possible.

1. Theologically unique among social ministries, advocacy for justice is grounded more in a God of justice than love, more in issues than in personal relationships. These Christians were motivated to act not because it was popular, but because it was right. You should not be surprised, then, to find the strongest commitment to justice among those who are more highly educated, think systemically, and live with less fear of retaliation.

2. In typical churches, members who strongly support social justice ministries are relatively unique and apparently accept their paradox. In a privileged class, they practice solidarity with the oppressed; in a spiritual group, they care about changing the world; as members of an institution, they advocate institutional change. They are known and respected in their congregations as people of integrity, yet a bit different from the rest.

3. Even when churches become involved in advocacy efforts, few congregations sustain the campaign over time. You may discover that justice ministries often precipitate stress among the leaders, and tension between the church and the community. Churches must be comfortable with conflict (an oxymoron?) if they are to continue in ministries that advocate community change.

Despite all these limitations, some typical churches adopted justice ministries. In our experience every church has some members who would support social change in a just cause with trusted leaders. In most churches you will find a few such members who are often a distinct but determined minority. *In practice you can initiate advocacy ministries by articulating the vision of a better world and legitimating members who are committed to trying to change the oppressive policies and procedures of existing institutions*, including schools, courts, corporations, and, yes, even (especially?) churches.

About the Unchosen Ministries

Of the six areas offered in project guidelines, participating congregations specifically focused on only two issues, education and housing. Their other choices (elderly, community, and justice) combined multiple issues in particular settings. To make their choices, churches asked the same kinds of questions that might affect your choice as well: Is it consistent with their faith (Does God want it done?)? Would it make any differ-ence? And could they imagine themselves doing it?

Two popular ministries were rejected because they did not fit the criteria. Churches believed hunger programs were needed, and they could imagine doing them, for example, yet no soup kitchens, hot meals, or food pantry programs were offered. When asked, congregational leaders suggested that such programs are too small and short term; they hoped to have a more lasting impact.

World peace stood at the other end of the spectrum. Peace is a bibli-cal goal and well worth attaining, but effecting peace is beyond the imag-ination of most church members. Two congregations within the Church of the Brethren explored a variety of international ministries working for peace. In the end they followed a similar theme in their heritage, creat-ing ministries of reconciliation that seek systemic changes in local in-stitutions, one in the schools and the other in the courts (see the appen-dix).

Employment and health ministries were also explored but not de-veloped by participating congregations. Models for such ministries exist in their communities with enthusiastic support from other congregations. Church and Community congregations saw these ministries as signifi-cant, but guided by professionals without comparable lay participation. You can launch these ministries in communities where the need is re-cognized and resources are available, conditions that did not occur among us.

Ministry Costs and Benefits

From these experiences of others, you may see the risks, costs, and im-pact of these ministries in your congregations and communities.

You can begin with educational concerns as an initial, natural bridge

for most congregations to launch social ministries. Educational procedures are widely known, resources are available, and congregations take
pride in their efforts. You can see the results in student growth and
teacher participation, but of course, lasting impact for all exceeds our
immediate evaluation.

You can initiate elderly programs in almost every community in
response to recognized needs. The cost of launching programs is usually
higher and more complex than first appears, but positive results build a
stronger family sense throughout the church.

You can develop comprehensive community programs that embrace
the fragments of a broken society, based on a renewal of parish theology
that improves the quality of life for everyone in your community.

You can build ministries in housing, health, employment, and other
more sophisticated programs when you assemble the specialized personnel and essential resources. For churches with the energy and expertise,
these ministries have a major impact in both the community and the
congregation.

You can mobilize the distinctive minority of members to advocate
for social justice when you share a vision for a better world and legitimate those most concerned as catalysts for social change. Although a
few congregations will make this ministry central, many will support
justice as one among several expressions of social concern.

Readers with interests in particular kinds of ministry can find more
information from descriptions, stories, and statistical reports on specific
programs in the appendix. Common to all successful programs are the
tenacious passion of a few people who care, the flexibility to make the
most of each opportunity, and the good humor to absorb the bumps as
each ministry unfolds in challenging unpredictability.

APPENDIX

Stories and Status of Church and Community Ministries

Susan E. Sporte

This appendix contains a five-year follow-up to twenty-five church-based community ministries that are described in an alphabetical listing in *Basic Steps toward Community Ministry* (The Alban Institute, 1991). Here we have clustered the ministries with similar themes and listed them in order of general interest, first education (nine ministries), followed by programs focused on elderly (four, including one lost and one gained), housing (four), community improvement (five), and advocating justice (four). After noting briefly the purpose of the ministry, we tried to catch the spirit or story of their work, and concluded with a few statistical comparisons on numbers of volunteers, staff, and budget. We further note the change in these ministries since the conclusion of seed funding in 1991 to the fall of 1995, distinguishing those that have stabilized (*), closed (-), grown less than 25 percent (+), and grown more than 25 percent (++).

A word of caution: No statistical standards can reflect the differences that are inherent in a wide variety of programs and the challenges faced in each separate situation. For example, you should not read these numbers as suggesting that a $1 million housing program is more important than a small budget to support volunteers in after-school tutoring. Further, we did not include the complex but very significant in-kind contributions, which would substantially alter the profile of these programs. In addition, we did not define the frequency or intensity of participation, since some volunteers and/or participants attend daily, some weekly, and some only on special occasions. In short, beware of comparisons, but enjoy the insight that each separate program provides.

I. Education: Nine Ministries

++*Kaleidoscope* of Indianapolis sponsors a Youth Center and teaches
mediation skills for young people at risk, particularly gang members.
They survived a major staff transition when the founding director re-
signed due to failing health. They have a Youth Diversion program,
working with a group of juvenile first-time criminal offenders, and have
had some success, particularly in getting participants in the program who
are from rival gangs to at least sit down at the same table and talk. They
are also doing a summer youth program with arts and crafts and cultural
arts. They have widened board representation to include new members
from the community and from other social service agencies, and some of
these board members bring a tough "bottom line" mentality about finances and programs that can conflict with the philosophy of board
members from the churches. Approximate annual budget $310,000; 25
volunteers, 9 full-time, 3 part-time staff; 240 participants, plus school
training programs.

+*Literacy Coalition* provides tutors for adult literacy in Kokomo,
Indiana, working mainly with those who are below adult basic educational levels. These tutors work with 75 people each month, with about
12 new placements monthly. As the most visible and active literacy
program in the area, they have become the "spearhead" for involving
others in a larger effort and seek to build a coalition with schools, local
corporations, and the resources of Indiana University. They have become a successful membership organization, made more secure with
funding from the United Way. They are considering expanding in the
areas of literacy for English-speaking migrant workers and in doing some
tutoring in the new county jail. The sheriff's department has also approached them about doing some work in the juvenile detention facility.
As the director says, "I think we're here to stay." Approximate annual
budget $60,000; 225 volunteers, 1 full-time, 2 part-time staff; 150
program participants per year.

+*Neighborhood Youth Outreach* is a youth program for tutoring, recreation, cultural expression, and college prep, also on the near north side
of Indianapolis. It has been difficult to secure a permanent full-time director, and the program currently employs 4 part-time people. They have

initiated a new summer program, providing meals, swimming, open gym, community service, and field trips for a clientele that includes grade school kids as well as teens. They are hoping to affiliate with Catholic Social Services to provide some basic funding levels. There has been an increase in the number of young women the program serves. They secured a grant for $30,000 annually from Lilly for the next two years, and the board finance committee is actively seeking additional support. Approximate annual budget $63,000; 12 volunteers, 4 staff members, each working about 30 hours per week; 230 participants.

In Peoria, Illinois, *CAPS* (Children and Parent Support) provides transportation for teen moms and their children to day care, school, and back home. The group also coordinates Parents of Rebellious Teens (PORT) support groups and works throughout the community to make teen mothers aware of the services available to them. They hope to become more proactive in girls' lives rather than just provide transport and now require participating teen parents to attend some form of parenting education. As an independent program it has recently relocated from the church to the YWCA building. Approximate annual budget $45,000; 25 volunteers, 2 part-time staff, and 2 part-time bus drivers; 60 PORT participants, 50 transport participants.

++*Hispanic Education Center* in downtown Indianapolis works with cultural transition, especially language, with students from Arsenal Tech High School and IUPUI (Indiana University and Purdue University at Indianapolis). It has served as a satellite center for some IUPUI classes. When they moved to St. Patrick's there was a period when they were unable to pay their agreed upon rental fees. The church did not pressure them, but project leaders felt it was a matter of conscience to repay. Recently, they added after-school enrichment programs and computer classes and received a grant for juvenile delinquency prevention. The center has a new summer program, which includes course work in math, English, and Spanish, as well as computer work, crafts, and cultural enrichment. There are 46 kids enrolled in this six-week program. Approximate annual budget, including staff and new programs, $150,000; 80 volunteers, 2.5 staff, plus some stipends for baby-sitting and summer teaching; 380 participants annually.

STEEP (Student Triumvirate Education Empowerment Program) provides after-school enrichment and tutoring for 20 plus students on two
afternoons a week in Chicago. They have also begun workshops for the
parents of the kids in their program. The program was initiated with
third graders, but after the first year, they found out that many of their
"graduates" wanted to stay, so they expanded, with the greatest interest
and need from kids in fourth grade. STEEP is largely a volunteer effort,
where the coordinator gets a stipend, and all others, including the bus
drivers, are volunteers. The local school principal is very enthusiastic,
and community support is strong, including a silent auction that raised
more than $4,000. Church involvement is clear in the number of STEEP
kids who attend Sunday school at Martin Temple and even recruit some
of their non-STEEP friends to the church. Approximate annual budget
$18,000; 36 volunteers, 1 stipend; 31 youth participants.

++*Strive* offers after-school tutoring in close cooperation with a neighboring elementary school on Chicago's south side. Primary funding
comes from the Southern Baptist Alliance, but they are actively raising
money through events and contributions. They try to provide continuity
of time between student and tutor. The once full-time director continues
on a part-time basis and additional church volunteers have been secured.
Church members remain committed, but as a small congregation (fewer
than 50 members) the church must allocate energy carefully. Approximate annual budget $35,000; 50 volunteers, 1 part-time staff; 50 youth
participants.

Riverside Park Church and Community Project renovated the church
building to make it user-friendly for after-school tutoring, recreation, and
a serious snack for elementary school kids in an African-American
neighborhood of Indianapolis. They have about 30 regular students, who
like it so much that they will return even after they have been suspended
for breaking the rules. Using mostly volunteer leaders, they are struggling to get parents involved and to find modest funds to keep very part-
time coordinators employed. The chairperson says, "We're hanging on
by a thread." They have been turned down on some recent grant applica-
tions and do not know where further funding will come from. They have
recently moved out of the church and into a nearby community center,
where the program continues. Approximate annual budget $15,000; 12
volunteers, 4 stipends; 38 youth participants.

Burnettsville Youth Board, in the small town of Burnettsville, Indiana, has had difficulty maintaining participation in an after-school latchkey program. With staff changes and good weather, participation declined drastically. The age group they were serving found other activities, and parents did not think that the daily program was necessary. Now the Youth Board plans monthly special activities—Santa Claus on a fire truck, Community Skating Party at the Bee Hive, etc., which have been well attended and which have maintained community support. Their most recent project is renovating the town park, which has become a community-wide effort. There will be a new slide and, for the first time ever, baby swings. The park will be dedicated at a celebration complete with a kids versus parents ball game. People are still supporting the efforts of this group, and they continue raising modest sums of money through an annual noodle supper and various raffles. Approximate annual budget $2,000; 4 regular volunteers, assisted by at least 10 others this year; 80 average attendance at their special events.

II. Elderly: Four Ministries

Three continuing, since one dissolved and one was reborn.

++*Caring Community* in Indianapolis provides an Adult Day Care Center in partnership with Catholic Social Services. It also provides respite care for elderly people and has begun an after-school enrichment program. This after-school program is operating at maximum capacity, with positive racial-ethnic mix, and without publicity, suggesting that it is meeting a significant need. There is a new summer program using donated land, where senior citizens teach youngsters about gardening. They continue to work for clear focus and for more volunteers, especially in respite care, and they are working to secure still more volunteers through the churches to provide home repair and housekeeping assistance for elderly people. Approximate annual budget $41,000. Catholic Social Services' budget for the Caring Place (adult day care center) is $250,000, to which the Caring Community contributes on a declining basis; 175 volunteers, 2 part-time staff; 25 respite care participants, 50 other elderly in day care; 20 children participants.

Christian Service Program, in the town of Canton, Illinois, serves elderly people by filling out medical insurance forms, helping with income tax forms, delivering community information, and so on. The number of users continues to increase, and the program's reputation continues to grow. Although sponsored by both Catholic and Congregational churches, most of the financial support at present comes from the United Church of Christ. The congregation continues to grant at least $10,000, and they receive another $3,000 from other UCC agencies. With strong financial and personal community support, they are revising their bylaws to include more board members from the community at large. Approximate annual budget $36,000; 30 volunteers, 2 part-time staff; 675 different clients in insurance needs and 600 people, with some duplication, in income tax preparation.

-*Daybreak*, offering day care and respite services in the community of Morton, Illinois, closed on November 1, 1992, with "not enough clients." In their evaluation they cited insufficient publicity and family pride that resists programs for elderly people until they are hospitalized as causes for their closure. It is included here because it is the only program that closed in the first year after the end of the seed funding in June 1991.

+*Irvington Senior Center*, offering hot meals, activities, and a gathering place for senior citizens on the east side of Indianapolis, closed in 1991 when the board did not find sufficient funding. The participants, however, organized themselves into a research effort until they located a YMCA that would house their program and then found their own funding from local agencies and businesses. Although we cannot claim their budget, staff, or volunteers, we applaud their tenacity for refusing to give up.

III. Housing: Four Ministries

++*Fountain Square Church and Community Project* of Indianapolis rehabilitates homes for low-income families and repairs homes for senior citizens, working with volunteers, probationers, and young people through the job apprentice program. They have merged with the Community Development Corporation (FSPCDC), and the new organization is called Southeast Neighborhood Development (SEND). This mix has raised questions about how to combine the values of a church-based organization with one that relies on professional contacts and that is more concerned with financial efficiency than with the lives of the people being served. The volunteer effort continues, with a number of groups returning for their fifth summer of work camps. The new organization greatly expands resources and productivity. They are now working on roughly 60 units a year with some sort of major repair and/or rehab. They have relocated, and the group may move again into Edwin Ray United Methodist Church, which was recently closed. Annual budget for combined organization about $2,200,000, for this ministry $744,000; 1,000 volunteer-hours per month, not counting board meetings; 8 full-time staff, many part-time on various funding programs; 120+ units of housing annually, including rental, owner-occupied repair, and acquisition-rehab-sale to new home owners.

++*PWHR* (Partners for Westside Housing Renewal) works with volunteers and paid staff to repair owner-occupied homes on Indianapolis's west side. The organization has merged with Westside Community Development Corporation, losing its separate identity, but greatly expanding its resources and impact. The name, PWHR, is still linked with project HOME to paint and repair homes during the summer using volunteers. Although the merger places a greater emphasis on repair efficiency over many volunteers, the budget, staff, and productivity have expanded as a result, without losing volunteers from several participating churches. PWHR's part of the annual budget $200,000; 20 regular volunteers, 200 work-camp volunteers; 4 staff; 208 owner-occupied rehabs for senior citizens, 50 owner-occupied rehabs, 13 rental units, 10 units for new home owners.

++*Lafayette Transitional Housing* provides transitional housing for families in Lafayette, Indiana. They have moved from their downtown location to a large older home with outside play space for children in residence. In addition to the six families in residence, there are four two-bedroom apartments and two single-family homes. They will be looking for another HUD grant, possibly to extend to people with special transitional needs such as people with AIDS, the elderly, or battered women. Their annual report shows some impressive statistics—e.g., 82 percent of "their" kids on the honor roll, 93 percent of those who leave are able to find and keep permanent housing, etc. With an energetic and committed board, they are finding additional resources through Purdue University. Approximate budget $218,000; 100 volunteers, 7 full-time, 2 part-time, and 3 temporary part-time staff; 250+ participants per year, including preresidential, housing, case management, and postresidential programs.

+*Wellspring* provides transitional housing for abused women and their children in a south Chicago community. With United Way funding for this year, they have hired a new director and are now operating at full capacity for their facility. They are challenged to expand representation and participation on their board and have recently added 4 more new members. They are also looking to broaden their funding base beyond their connections in the Evangelical Covenant Church and have been successful in getting financial assistance from a local Methodist church and the Lady Lions. They have added more program components, including a volunteer who works as a substance abuse counselor. They have been rewriting their mission statement so it is clear that they are acting as more than "landlords." Approximate annual budget $80,000; 125 volunteers, some for one-time needs, 1 full-time staff; 40 participants last year.

IV. Community Improvement: Five Ministries

++*C.A.R.E.* Center in Chicago considers itself a complete outreach program of Sweet Holy Spirit Baptist Church. They have programs ranging from ROCK (Reclaiming Our Community and Kids) and YES (Youth Extended Summer) to AA, food giveaway, tutoring, GED, and delivering cooked meals to people on the street. They have 15 young people paid by the city working this summer in many of these programs. The church continues to grow—for example, they baptized 32 kids and 53 adults on a recent Sunday. The bulk of their budget comes from free will offerings from the congregation, although they also receive support from the Southern Baptists and from area merchants. The director says, "It takes lots of prayer, lots of faith, lots of praise—and a lot of volunteers." Approximate annual budget $45,000; 40 volunteers, 2 full-time staff; countless families per month for food, 150 kids per week for various programs.

Mustard Seed counsels and supports families while it works for self-sufficiency in Tipton, Indiana. Now that community social service agencies have come to see this program as complementary, it has become a recognized agency in the service network. With good service, they now have a waiting list and have received referrals from Welfare and Vocational Rehabilitation. For the first time they have a balance of about $12,000 (received primarily from a single bequest), and are beneficiaries of the Presbyterian Hunger Fund. Seven churches are now active partners, and they are also working closely with a new chapter of Habitat for Humanity in town. Approximate annual budget $18,000; 8 volunteers, 1 part-time staff; about 30 participants (8 families) annually.

-*Bradford Church and Community Project* provides employment for teenagers doing maintenance and lawn work in Bradford, Illinois. The project purchased a computer on which the youth compose a community newsletter, with ads from local businesses, that is mailed to 639 people monthly. They have become more like a business themselves—this computer allows them to bill people rather than needing payment for work at the time of completion. In 1993, the budget was $20,000; 12 regular volunteers plus volunteer equipment maintenance, 4 part-time staff; 30 youth employed. But the project closed in 1994. One pastor said, "It was the best thing that happened here in years, but four small town churches just couldn't keep it going."

Lacon Community Center, in Lacon, Illinois, is a newly constructed facility in the center of town that offers lunches and program for senior citizens, nursery school, teen dances, and a variety of other community-sponsored activities, such as exercise classes, crafts show, and others. Head Start moved out in the winter, partly due to the noise of the kids competing with the quiet of the seniors' group. Their last major construction effort, installing flooring over the concrete floor, was recently completed by volunteers. Teen dances are especially popular, and senior programs remain strong. The community newsletter is widely distributed, keeping people informed. The churches and church members remain the primary support for the program. Approximate annual budget for the Center $15,700; 20 volunteers, 1 part-time staff; 20 participants in seniors' programs, 80 in youth dances, 20 in preschool, plus each program has budget and staff.

*ACDC (Active Care Develops Community) has given focus to the energy of Deer Creek, Indiana, to construct a community center. Unfortunately, construction was delayed due to official conflict over septic/ sewer connections. The work has been completed, the kitchen is in, and the group hosted its first monthly pancake breakfast in the building in June. They envision more educational events and will probably create a recycling center on the grounds. They anticipate a space where kids can play softball and volleyball—this is currently being worked on. The project is also still working on obtaining clear 501(c)3 status, rather than 501(c)4 (civic organization). The Lacon model makes it look easy, and it is not. Approximate budget $15,000; 100 volunteers in various projects that touch the lives of almost everyone in town. Since the goal of the ministry was a new sense of community, program is limited only by the imagination of participants.

V. Advocacy: Four Ministries

+Hope for the Nineties advocates multiple use of church buildings through a partnership of Hope Presbyterian Church with St. John's Hospital Adult Day Care, Parent Place, and Interfaith Counseling Center in Springfield, Illinois. These agencies share church space to provide day care for Alzheimer's patients, child abuse prevention, parenting education, family counseling, and congregational worship and church activities. Although each is an independent organization, together they share their resources, joys, and struggles. The most tension surrounds a loan from the church to one agency, which the church cannot afford to carry and the agency is finding difficult to repay. Programs are going well for all groups, and all seem able to weather staff and program transitions. Approximate gross budget for three programs $500,000, not including St. John's Adult Day Care; 35 church members volunteer in at least one of the other agencies; Parent Place served 150 kids and 831 adults; Interfaith had 1,200 client-hours; the church membership has increased 30 percent since the project began; St. John's program withdrew in 1995, and the board is planning to replace it with another agency for the elderly.

HANDS is an active advocacy agency for deaf and hearing impaired people in Chicago, Illinois. As affirmation, they recently received a second $25,000 grant from DORS (Department of Rehabilitative Services) to help inform hearing impaired people of their rights under the ADA (Americans with Disabilities Act). The director provides strong leadership in Springfield to ensure the phone Relay Service continues in the way that best serves the deaf community. They have been able to expand their office facilities, add additional staff, and work with agencies like police departments where interpreters and TTY accessibility are mandated by law. They will expand to work with senior citizens in the retirement needs of hearing impaired people, and they are expanding their base with workshops such as "How to Protect Against Being a Victim." They are increasingly seen as a grassroots organization that will be heard, for hearing impaired people. Approximate annual budget $50,000; 35 volunteers, 1 staff; 500 participants (400 members).

++*ECR* (Education for Conflict Resolution) provides mediation and re-conciliation training in the elementary schools, mediation training for churches and other groups, divorce/custody mediation boards, and community board hearings in North Manchester, Indiana. Although initially anchored in the local schools, the director and trained volunteers are doing an increasing number of school trainings in other places on a fee schedule. They are also beginning training programs with ELCA and other regional church groups. Unfortunately, payment from training is slow, so they are constantly in precarious financial condition. They receive some staff help through student interns from Manchester College, and have a "Green Thumb" worker (low-income worker aged at least 55 paid for by the state). The director reflects the group, saying, "We might run out of money, but we won't quit." Approximate annual budget $85,000; 105 volunteers, 2 part-time staff. With requests from all over the state, they have opened branch offices in Fort Wayne and Huntington and registered training for 500+ school leaders, 400+ leaders in community and family mediation.

Mediation Services of Tippecanoe County offers victim-offender mediation as an alternative to normal court procedure, and a school mediation program in Lafayette, Indiana. With each new probation officer, they must re-win the confidence of the court, but with only a part-time director they live on fees for services, along with occasional donations. Their conflict manager program in local schools is going well, and they are expanding to develop mediation training programs based on their current work with groups of employees from local businesses. In addition to the Church of the Brethren and Mennonites, the Assembly of God Church has joined, board members have been attracted from the community, and they receive financial support from Central Presbyterian Church. The director says, "We need more people and more time and more money, but we intend to be around." Approximate budget $23,000; 20 volunteers, 1 part-time staff; have trained 40+ mediators this year for work with both schools and court referrals.

EPILOGUE

No summary could do justice to the hard-won insights of these ministries, but a few words of appreciation, celebration, and encouragement are in order. In these experiences we find good news for those who believe that God calls and strengthens Christians in community ministry. We did not always find what we expected, but what we found was better than we had dared to hope.

In the Church and Community Project, we bet right when we built ministries around lay leaders. Church leaders—members and clergy together—made these ministries happen, and the members brought far more interest and commitment than most clergy anticipated. In the process we challenged many old myths that continue to inhibit others from developing community ministries.

We expected churches to be interested in issues, and found that they cared passionately about people, neighbors they did not know, when they shared the pain and believed that a ministry could make a difference. We expected projects to be something new, and discovered that ministries grew from selected use of past experiences. We expected to train leaders, and found that we were coaching ordinary people who became leaders because they believed in what they were doing. We were told that there is a right way to organize, and found radically different styles that are effective when people want the job to get done.

We were afraid that we could not find the resources for ministry without undermining existing budgets. The problem is genuine, but with effort and imagination the leaders of these ministries found tens and even hundreds of thousands of dollars—even church people who "hated to ask for money" could do it. We predicted that quiet, comfortable churches could not engage in justice ministry, and found that righteous anger and social change were often irrepressible. We expected partners to expand ministry, and found that they often complicated the task—yet participants said that partners are "worth it" when leaders work at bridging differences without losing their unique commitments. For many, these new relationships were a surprise reward to their ministries.

We were warned that if congregations were distracted by social ministry, they would decline in membership or dissipate spiritual commitment, and we found that lively churches have energy in all dimensions—worship and education, spiritual growth and fellowship, evangelism and social ministry. Especially we had hoped that participants would report a growth in faith, and to our initial disappointment, we found no change in what they believed, whether members, pastors, or denominational leaders. But we did find that they discovered a profound satisfaction in living their faith-in-action, and this feeling increased in direct proportion to their personal participation in community ministries.

Leaders worked hard for the lessons they learned. In visiting these ministries, Sue Sporte remembers a typical comment of an exhausted volunteer, "We've learned a lot about the tenacity of faith." However, no one said, "We wish we hadn't started this." The overwhelming consensus was, "Even if we stop tomorrow, we've done a lot, we've learned a lot, and we've received even more." As a member at Martin Temple put it, "My advice to anyone is, 'It's worth the risk. Just go for it.'"

REFERENCES

Chapter 1

Johnson, Susanne. Citing George Lindbeck in *Christian Spiritual Formation in the Church and Classroom*. Nashville: Abingdon Press, 1989, p. 148.

Chapter 3

Carroll, Lewis. *Through the Looking Glass*. New York: Bantam, 1988, p. 157.

Drucker, Peter F. *The Practice of Management*. New York: Harper and Row, 1986, p. 158.

Dudley, Carl S., and Sally A. Johnson. *Energizing the Congregation: Images that Shape Your Church's Ministry*. Louisville: Westminster/ John Knox, 1993, p. 63.

Martin, Joanne, and M. Paivers. "More Vivid and Persuasive than Quantitative Data." In *Psychological Foundation of Organizational Behavior*, edited by B. W. Staw. Glenview, Ill.: Scott Foresman, 1981, pp. 161-68.

Senge, Peter. *The Fifth Discipline*. New York: Doubleday Currency, 1990, pp. 205-6.

Chapter 8

Gates, Henry Louis, Jr. Review of *Culture of Complaint. New Yorker*, April 10, 1993, p. 113.

McCarthy, David B. "The Emerging Importance of Presbyterian Polity." In *The Organizational Revolution: Presbyterians and American Denominationalism*, edited by Milton J. Coalter, John Mulder, and Lewis Weeks. Louisville: Westminster/John Knox, 1992, p. 279.

Pope, Liston. *Millhands and Preachers*. New Haven: Yale University Press, 1942, pp. 70-116.

Roof, Wade Clark. *Generation of Seekers: The Spiritual Journeys of the Baby Boomer Generation*. San Francisco: Harper Collins, 1993, p. 245.

Williams, Newell, ed. *A Case Study of Mainstream Protestantism*. Grand Rapids: Eerdmans,1991, pp. 561f.

The Alban Institute:
an invitation to membership

The Alban Institute, begun in 1974, believes that the congregation is essential to the task of equipping the people of God to minister in the church and the world. A multi-denominational membership organization, the Institute provides on-site training, educational programs, consulting, research, and publishing for hundreds of churches across the country.

The Alban Institute invites you to be a member of this partnership of laity, clergy, and executives–a partnership that brings together people who are raising important questions about congregational life and people who are trying new solutions, making new discoveries, finding a new way of getting clear about the task of ministry. The Institute exists to provide you with the kinds of information and resources you need to support your ministries.

Join us now and enjoy these benefits:

CONGREGATIONS: The Alban Journal, a highly respected journal published six times a year, to keep you up to date on current issues and trends.

Inside Information, Alban's quarterly newsletter, keeps you informed about research and other happenings around Alban. Available to members only.

Publications Discounts:

- ☐ 15% for Individual, Retired Clergy, and Seminarian Members
- ☐ 25% for Congregational Members
- ☐ 40% for Judicatory and Seminary Executive Members

Discounts on Training and Education Events

Write our Membership Department at the address below or call us at 1-800-486-1318 or 301-718-4407 for more information about how to join The Alban Institute's growing membership, particularly about Congregational Membership in which 12 designated persons receive all benefits of membership.

 The Alban Institute, Inc.
Suite 433 North
4550 Montgomery Avenue
Bethesda, MD 20814-3341